KU-114-132

WITHDRAWN

2006 | Higher | New Arrangements

[BLANK PAGE]

X213/301

NATIONAL QUALIFICATIONS 2006	FRIDAY, 26 MAY 1.00 PM – 2.50 PM	RELIGIOUS, MORAL AND PHILOSOPHICAL STUDIES HIGHER Paper 1

There are two Sections in this paper:

Section 1 – Morality in the Modern World
Section 2 – Christianity: Belief and Science

Section 1 – You should answer **two** questions: Question 1 and **one** from **either**
Question 2 – Gender **or**
Question 3 – Crime and Punishment **or**
Question 4 – Medical Ethics **or**
Question 5 – War and Peace.

Section 2 has **one** question. You should answer all parts of this question.

The skills of knowledge and understanding (KU) and analysis and evaluation (AE) are being assessed in this paper. When answering each question you should note the number of marks allocated to each skill and use this information as a guide to the length and type of answer required.

SCOTTISH
QUALIFICATIONS
AUTHORITY

SA X213/301 6/3670

SECTION 1

Marks   Code

Morality in the Modern World

You **must** answer **Question 1 (*a – c*)** and **one** other question (**either** 2 **or** 3
or 4 **or** 5)

Question 1

Instructions: Answer **all** parts of the question **(*a*) – (*c*)**. The number of marks available can be found at the end of each question. You should use these as a guide to the amount of detail you should include in your answer.

(*a*) What is meant by the claim that moral values are heteronomous?   **2**   **KU**

(*b*) Explain the role of reason as a source of moral guidance in **one** or **more**
religion(s) you have studied.   **3**   **KU**

(*c*) Describe the key features of Virtue Ethics.   **5**   **KU**

(10)

Question 2 – Gender

Marks   Code

Reminder: *You should answer this question if you have studied **Gender Issues** in the Morality in the Modern World Unit.*

Instructions: Read the statement below then answer **all** parts of the question **(a) – (d)**. The number of marks available for each part of the question is indicated. You should use this as a guide to the amount of detail you should include in your answer.

> ### Statement:
>
> "Stereotypes pigeonhole boys and girls, men and women into fixed roles and behaviours that deny individual aspirations. They limit what both males and females can do. In effect, these stereotypes force us to be what others want us to be. We should be free to choose our own life goals and roles."

(a) Describe how **one** religion might be considered to have stereotyped the roles of men and women.

3   KU

(b) What distinctive contribution might women make to a religion?

4   2KU
    2AE

(c) Explain how gender stereotyping might create problems in society.

8   2KU
    6AE

(d) *"Equality of opportunity is something that everyone should support."*

Discuss **two** responses to this statement, at least one of which should be religious.

15   4KU
     11AE

(30)

[Turn over

Question 3 – Crime and Punishment

Marks Code

Reminder: *You should answer this question if you have studied* **Crime and Punishment** *in the Morality in the Modern World Unit.*

Instructions: Read the following Case Study then answer **all** parts of the question *(a) – (d)*. The number of marks available for each part of the question is indicated. You should use this as a guide to the amount of detail you should give in your answer.

Case Study

The jury found the accused guilty of murder.

Before passing sentence, the judge described the killer as a bitter and twisted man, a cold blooded murderer who had killed for no reason.

He described the various purposes of punishment and pointed out that reformation of the criminal would be a very unlikely outcome of the punishment given in this particular case.

Then, looking directly at the man in the dock, the judge told him that because of the nature of his crime he considered him to be a severe danger to the public and that he had no alternative but to impose a sentence of life imprisonment.

(a) The judge might punish for the purpose of deterrence or reformation.

Describe fully what is meant by deterrence and reformation.   6   KU

(b) State the advantages of community service as a form of punishment.   4   KU

(c) What moral issues are raised by imprisoning a person for life?   5   AE

(d) *"Retribution is not an acceptable reason for punishment."*

Discuss **two** responses to this statement, at least one of which should be religious.   15   AE

(30)

Question 4 – Medical Ethics

Marks   Code

Reminder: *You should answer this question if you have studied* **Medical Ethics** *in the Morality in the Modern World Unit.*

Instructions: Read the following Case Study then answer **all** parts of the question **(a) – (d)**. The number of marks available for each part of the question is indicated. You should use this as a guide to the amount of detail you should give in your answer.

Case Study

A happy occasion, a baby has just been born! However, this is no ordinary baby. The parents of this child want to use stem cells from his umbilical cord to treat his older brother who has a life threatening blood disorder.

The baby, called Jamie, was genetically selected as an embryo to be a near perfect match for his 4 year old brother. In addition to this the baby has not been born in the UK but in America, as the vital test tube treatment that is required for this procedure is not legal in the UK.

(a) The case study refers to therapeutic genetic engineering. Describe **one** other purpose of genetic engineering.   **3   KU**

(b) Explain what the law in the UK says about genetic engineering.   **6   KU**

(c) Explain the moral issues raised by the case study.   **6   AE**

(d) *"Whilst recognising the benefits of genetic engineering we must be careful not to think that because we **can** do it we **ought** to do it."*

   Discuss **two** responses to this statement, at least one of which should be religious.   **15   AE**

(30)

[Turn over

Question 5 – War and Peace   *Marks*   *Code*

Reminder: *You should answer this question if you have studied* **War and Peace** *in the Morality in the Modern World Unit.*

Instructions: Read the following extract then answer **all** parts of the question *(a) – (d)*. The number of marks available for each part of the question is indicated. You should use this as a guide to the amount of detail you should give in your answer.

> *Extract*
>
> Smart missiles have a number of advantages over other weapons. First deployed in 1990, they have been used increasingly in recent warfare. It is not, however, these conventional weapons that raise the most serious moral issues for our world. It is the possession and use of non-conventional weapons.

(a) What advantages might "smart" missiles have over other weapons?   **3**   **KU**

(b) Describe how International Conventions have tried to restrict the use of weapons.   **3**   **KU**

(c) What moral issues might be raised by the use of conventional weapons?   **9**   **2KU**
                                                                                              7AE

(d) *"It is morally justifiable for a country to possess weapons of mass destruction."*

Discuss **two** responses to this statement, at least one of which should be religious.   **15**   **3KU**
                                                                                                        12AE

                                                                                                        (30)

[END OF SECTION 1]

SECTION 2

Marks   Code

Christianity: Belief and Science

Instructions: Read the following extract then answer **all** parts of the question **(a) – (f)**. The number of marks available for each question is indicated. You should use these as a guide to the amount of detail you should give in your answer.

Extract:

For many people today the challenge to religious belief arises from the assumption that the scientific method is the only road to knowledge.

There is no doubt that the success of science has been due to a large extent to the methods it uses in its search for truth.

Religion, on the other hand, has relied on different sources of knowledge—mainly revelation, but also reasoned argument based on observation of nature. It has been said that scientific method is a more reliable source of knowledge than revelation.

(a) What methods does science use in its search for truth?   6   KU

(b) Explain the importance of revelation for Christians.   6   2KU
                                                                                                  4AE

(c) What limitations might there be in both scientific method and revelation?   6   AE

(d) Explain how the Teleological Argument uses observation of the world to support Christian belief in God.   8   4KU
                                                                                                  4AE

(e) Describe the key features of evolutionary theory.   4   KU

(f) *"For some Christians there is no contradiction in believing that God created human life and also believing in the theory of evolution."*

Can this claim be justified?   10   3KU
                                                                                                  7AE

(40)

[END OF SECTION 2]

[END OF QUESTION PAPER]

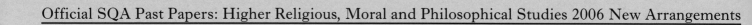

[BLANK PAGE]

X213/302

NATIONAL QUALIFICATIONS 2006	FRIDAY, 26 MAY 3.10 PM – 4.00 PM	RELIGIOUS, MORAL AND PHILOSOPHICAL STUDIES HIGHER Paper 2

You should answer **either**

Section 1:   Buddhism

or

Section 2:   Christianity

or

Section 3:   Hinduism

or

Section 4:   Islam

or

Section 5:   Judaism

or

Section 6:   Sikhism

The skills of knowledge and understanding (KU) and analysis and evaluation (AE) are being assessed in this paper. When answering each question you should note the number of marks allocated to each skill and use this information as a guide to the length and type of answer required.

SA X213/302 6/3670

SCOTTISH QUALIFICATIONS AUTHORITY
©

Section 1 – Buddhism   *Marks   Code*

Reminder: *You should choose this section if you have studied* **Buddhism** *in the World Religion Unit. Answer* **BOTH** *questions (1 and 2) in this section of the paper.*

Question 1

Instructions: *Read the following source then answer* **all** *parts of Question 1 (a) – (e). The number of marks available for each part is indicated. Use these as a guide to the amount of detail you should include in your answer.*

Source

He who is free from credulous beliefs since he has seen the eternal nirvana, who has thrown off the bondage of the lower life and, far beyond temptations, has surrendered all his desires, he is indeed great amongst men.

Wherever holy men dwell, that is indeed a place of joy—be it in the village or in a forest or in a valley or in the hills. They make delightful the forests where other people could not dwell. Because they have not the burden of desires, they have that joy which others find not.

Dhammapada 97-99

(a) Describe what Buddhists understand by "eternal nirvana".   4   **KU**

(b) "*. . . bondage of the lower life. . .*"

Explain what Buddhists would understand by this phrase.   5   **KU**

(c) Describe how desire and temptation played a part in the Buddha's life as he progressed towards Enlightenment.   4   **KU**

(d) Why is it important for Buddhists to surrender all desires?   4   **AE**

(e) "*Wherever holy men dwell, that is indeed a place of joy. . .*"

Is it necessary to be a monk to achieve enlightenment? Discuss with reference to two Buddhist traditions.   8   **AE**

(25)

Question 2   *Marks   Code*

Instructions: Read the **statement** below then answer the *question* that follows.

Statement:

"*It is a Buddhist's aim to cultivate peace, bliss and wellbeing in him/herself.*"

Discuss the extent to which belief in Anatta helps a Buddhist to achieve this aim.   **15   6KU**
                                                                                              9AE

                                                                                         (15)

                                                                                         (40)

                                                                     [Turn over

Section 2 – Christianity   *Marks   Code*

Reminder: *You should choose this section if you have studied **Christianity** in the World Religion Unit. Answer **BOTH** questions (**1** and **2**) in this section of the paper.*

Question 1

Instructions: *Read the following source then answer **all** parts of Question 1 (a) – (e). The number of marks available for each part is indicated. Use these as a guide to the amount of detail you should include in your answer.*

Source

But we do see Jesus, who for a little while was made lower than the angels, so that through God's grace he should die for everyone. We see him now crowned with glory and honour because of the death he suffered. It was only right that God, who creates and preserves all things, should make Jesus perfect through suffering, in order to bring many sons to share his glory. For Jesus is the one who leads them to salvation.

Hebrews **2: vv 9, 10**

(a) Describe the suffering of Jesus.   4   **KU**

(b) "*. . . because of the death he suffered.*"

In what ways do Christians remember the death of Jesus?   4   **KU**

(c) Explain why Christians think that it is important to develop their relationship with God.   6   **3KU**
                                                                               3AE

(d) "*. . . in order to bring many sons to share his glory.*"

Explain what Christians would understand by the phrase, "*share his glory.*"   7   **3KU**
                                                                               4AE

(e) "*For Jesus is the one who leads them to salvation.*"   4   **AE**

How important is this belief for Christians?   **(25)**

Question 2

Marks Code

Instructions: Read the **statement** below then answer the *question* that follows.

Statement:

"*Belief in final judgement helps Christians achieve the goals of life.*"

Discuss this belief with reference to **two** Christian traditions.

15 5KU
10AE

(15)
(40)

[Turn over

Section 3 – Hinduism   *Marks*   *Code*

Reminder: *You should choose this section if you have studied **Hinduism** in the World Religion Unit. Answer **BOTH** questions (**1** and **2**) in this section of the paper.*

Question 1

Instructions: *Read the following source then answer **all** parts of Question 1 (**a**) – (**e**). The number of marks available for each part is indicated. Use these as a guide to the amount of detail you should include in your answer.*

> *Source*
>
> "Those who in oneness worship thee as God immanent in all; and those who worship the Transcendent, the Imperishable—Of these, who are the best Yogis?"
>
> **Bhagavad Gita 12:1**

(*a*)   Explain what Hindus understand by the phrase "God immanent in all".   **3**   **KU**

(*b*)   Describe what some Hindus mean by God being "the Transcendent".   **3**   **KU**

(*c*)   Why, for some Hindus, is bhakti the most desirable path to follow?   **7**   **3KU**
                                                                                      4AE

(*d*)   *"Those who know, live by what is taught in the Vedas."*
                                                   Maitri Upanishad 7:10

What is the importance of the Vedas to Hindus?   **4**   **KU**

(*e*)   How essential is a guru in the life of Hindus?   **8**   **3KU**
                                                                5AE

                                                               (25)

Question 2   *Marks   Code*

Instructions: Read the **statement** below then answer the *question* that follows.

Statement:

"*To understand Hinduism you have to understand the importance of karma.*"

Is this an accurate assessment of the importance of karma?   **15   4KU**
                                                                                          11AE

                                                                                  (15)

                                                                                  (40)

                                                                      [Turn over

Section 4 – Islam   *Marks   Code*

Reminder: *You should choose this section if you have studied* **Islam** *in the World Religion Unit. Answer* **BOTH** *questions (***1** *and* **2***) in this section of the paper.*

Question 1

Instructions: *Read the following source then answer* **all** *parts of Question 1* **(a) – (e)**. *The number of marks available for each part is indicated. Use these as a guide to the amount of detail you should include in your answer.*

Source

. . . revealed before your time,—when ye give them their due dowers, and desire chastity, not lewdness, nor secret intrigues. If anyone rejects faith, fruitless is his work, and in the Hereafter he will be in the ranks of those who have lost (all spiritual good.)

O ye who believe! When ye prepare for prayer, wash your faces, and your hands (and arms) to the elbows; Rub your heads (with water); and (wash) your feet to the ankles. If ye are on a journey, or one of you cometh from offices of nature, or ye have been in contact with women, and ye find no water, then take for yourself clean sand or earth, and rub therewith your faces and hands, God doth not wish to place you in a difficulty, but to make you clean, and to complete his favour to you, that you may be grateful.

Surah 5 v 6-7

(a) "... *but to make you clean*. . ."

Describe what Muslims understand by this phrase.   3   KU

(b) What do Muslims consider to be the purpose of prayer?   4   KU

(c) Why is it important for a Muslim to submit to the will of Allah?   5   1KU
                                                                              4AE

(d) "*If anyone rejects faith, fruitless is his work, and in the Hereafter he will be in the ranks of those who have lost* . . ."

In what ways is this a significant passage for Muslims?   6   3KU
                                                                              3AE

(e) Why should Muslims be concerned about the use of free-will?   7   4KU
                                                                              3AE

                                                                            (25)

Question 2

Marks   Code

Instructions: Read the **statement** below then answer the *question* that follows.

Statement:

"*Muslims would agree that the Five Pillars are of benefit both to the individual and to the community of Islam.*"

Discuss with reference to **two** of the Pillars **other** than Prayer.

15   **4KU**
      11AE

(15)

(40)

[Turn over

Section 5 – Judaism   *Marks   Code*

Reminder: *You should choose this section if you have studied **Judaism** in the World Religion Unit. Answer **BOTH** questions (**1** and **2**) in this section of the paper.*

Question 1

Instructions: *Read the following source then answer **all** parts of Question 1 (**a**) – (**e**). The number of marks available for each part is indicated. Use these as a guide to the amount of detail you should include in your answer.*

> *Source*
>
> But in the end of days it shall come to pass, that the mountain of the LORD'S house shall be established as the top of the mountains, and it shall be exalted above the hills; and peoples shall flow unto it. And many nations shall go and say: 'Come ye, and let us go up to the mountain of the LORD, and to the house of the God of Jacob; and He will teach us of His ways, and we will walk in His paths'; for out of Zion shall go forth the law, and the word of the LORD from Jerusalem. And He shall judge between many peoples, and shall decide concerning mighty nations afar off; and they shall beat their swords into ploughshares, and their spears into pruning hooks; nation shall not lift up sword against nation, neither shall they learn war any more.
>
> ***Micah** 4: 1-3*

(*a*) *"But in the end of days it shall come to pass . . ."*

Describe Jewish beliefs about the Messianic Age.   5   **KU**

(*b*) *". . . and He will teach us of His ways . . ."*

In what ways do Jews observe the teachings of God in the home?   5   **KU**

(*c*) *". . . for out of Zion shall go forth the law. . ."*

Explain the connection between the Written Law and the Oral Law.   4   **2KU
2AE**

(*d*) Explain the importance of the principle of justice in Judaism.   4   **AE**

(*e*) Discuss the view that this world (Olam ha-Zeh) is more important to Jewish belief and practice than the world to come (Olam ha-Bah).   7   **3KU
4AE**

(25)

Question 2   *Marks   Code*

Instructions: Read the **statement** below then answer the ***question*** that follows.

Statement:

"Jews believe that human beings are created in the image of God."

Discuss the implications of this belief.   **15   5KU**

                                                                                                                10AE

                                                                                                                (15)

                                                                                                                (40)

                                                                                        [Turn over

Section 6 – Sikhism

Marks Code

Reminder: *You should choose this section if you have studied* **Sikhism** *in the World Religion Unit. Answer* **BOTH** *questions (* **1** *and* **2** *) in this section of the paper.*

Question 1

Instructions: *Read the following source then answer* **all** *parts of Question 1 (a) – (f). The number of marks available for each part is indicated. Use these as a guide to the amount of detail you should include in your answer.*

Source

Good karma has dawned for me—my Lord and Master has become merciful. I sing the kirtan of the Praises of the Lord, . . . My struggle is ended; I have found peace and tranquillity. All my wanderings have ceased . . . The Primal Lord, the Architect of Destiny has come into my conscious mind; I seek the Sanctuary of the Saints . . . Nanak sings the Praises of his Lord and Master; night and day he is lovingly focused on Him.

***Guru Granth Sahib,* 1000**

(*a*) In this source, God is referred to as the "Architect of Destiny".

What is meant by this title? 3 KU

(*b*) The main sacred text of the Sikh faith is called the Guru Granth Sahib.

Describe **two** other ways in which the title Guru is used by Sikhs. 4 KU

(*c*) *Singing "the kirtan of the Praises of the Lord" is one way in which Sikhs worship God.*

Describe **one** other way in which Sikhs worship God. 2 KU

(*d*) Explain the phrase "all my wanderings". 5 2KU
3AE

(*e*) Why is sewa important to Sikhs? 4 1KU
3AE

(*f*) This source helps to describe the final goal of life for Sikhs.

Explain Sikh beliefs about the final goal of life. 7 3KU
4AE

(25)

Question 2   *Marks   Code*

Instructions: Read the **statement** below then answer the *question* that follows.

Statement:

"*The need to fulfil the social duties of a householder could lead Sikhs away from reunion with God.*"

Would all Sikhs agree with this statement?   **15   5KU**

                                                                                                      10AE

                                                                                                      (15)

                                                                                                      (40)

[END OF QUESTION PAPER]

[BLANK PAGE]

[BLANK PAGE]

Official SQA Past Papers: Religious, Moral and Philosophical Studies 2007

X213/301

NATIONAL
QUALIFICATIONS
2007

FRIDAY, 25 MAY
1.00 PM – 2.45 PM

RELIGIOUS, MORAL
AND PHILOSOPHICAL
STUDIES
HIGHER
Paper 1

There are two Sections in this paper:

Section 1 – Morality in the Modern World
Section 2 – Christianity: Belief and Science

You should answer **two** questions from Section 1: Question 1 and **one** from **either**

Question 2 – Gender **or**
Question 3 – Crime and Punishment **or**
Question 4 – Medical Ethics **or**
Question 5 – War and Peace.

Section 2 has **one** mandatory question.

The skills of knowledge and understanding (KU) and analysis and evaluation (AE) are being assessed in this paper. When answering each question you should note the number of marks allocated to each skill as indicated after each part of the question.

SECTION 1

Marks   Code

Morality in the Modern World

You **must** answer **Question 1 (a) – (c)** and **one** other question (**either** 2 **or** 3 **or** 4 **or** 5)

Question 1

Instructions: Answer **all** parts of the question *(a) – (c)*. The number of marks available can be found at the end of each question. You should use these as a guide to the amount of detail you should include in your answer.

(*a*) Describe the Euthyphro dilemma.   **4   KU**

(*b*) What is the Golden Rule?   **2   KU**

(*c*) What are the key features of Utilitarian ethics?   **4   KU**

                                                                                                      (10)

Question 2 – Gender

Marks   Code

Reminder: *You should answer this question if you have studied **Gender Issues** in the Morality in the Modern World Unit.*

Instructions: Read the extract below then answer **all** parts of the question **(a)** – **(d)**. The number of marks available for each part of the question is indicated. You should use this as a guide to the amount of detail you should include in your answer.

Extract

"Throughout the twentieth century there were many developments in the UK that aimed to change the traditional economic relationships that exist between the sexes. Women are still earning less than men—but the gap is closing all the time."

(a) In what ways were women economically disadvantaged in the past?   **4   KU**

(b) How might economic equality between the sexes benefit men?   **4   AE**

(c) How successful have the guidelines provided by the Equal Opportunities
     Commission been in improving the economic situation of women?   **6   2KU**
                                                                                    4AE

(d) *"Economic inequality between men and women is morally unjustifiable."*

   (i) Describe **two** possible religious responses to this statement.

   (ii) Assess the strengths and weaknesses of these responses.   **16   4KU**
                                                                                    12AE

                                                                               (30)

[Turn over

Question 3 – Crime and Punishment   *Marks*   *Code*

Reminder: *You should answer this question if you have studied **Crime and Punishment** in the Morality in the Modern World Unit.*

Instructions: Read the following Case Study then answer **all** parts of the question **(a) – (d)**. The number of marks available for each part of the question is indicated. You should use this as a guide to the amount of detail you should give in your answer.

Case Study

"One of the most controversial cases in Britain was that of Timothy Evans. It raised a number of moral issues which ultimately led to the abolition of capital punishment in the United Kingdom. However, today, in the light of other prominent cases, some sections of society are once again calling for the reintroduction of the death penalty."

(a) Describe the main events surrounding the case of Timothy Evans.   3   **KU**

(b) How helpful is the United Nations Declaration of Human Rights in addressing the issue of Capital Punishment?   5   **2KU**
3AE

(c) *"All methods of execution are immoral."*

How might a non-religious person respond to this view?   6   **2KU**
4AE

(d) *"It is difficult to see how any religious person could justify capital punishment."*

(i) Describe **two** religious viewpoints supporting capital punishment.

(ii) What do you consider to be the strengths and weaknesses of each of the viewpoints?   16   **4KU**
12AE

(30)

Question 4 – Medical Ethics

Marks   Code

Reminder: *You should answer this question if you have studied* **Medical Ethics** *in the Morality in the Modern World Unit.*

Instructions: Read the following Case Study then answer **all** parts of the question **(a) – (d)**. The number of marks available for each part of the question is indicated. You should use this as a guide to the amount of detail you should give in your answer.

Case Study

John, 27, is permanently paralysed from the neck down as the result of a very bad car accident. He will be paralysed for the rest of his life and he does not want to live like this.

He has asked to be allowed to die.

(a) Describe the differences between voluntary and involuntary euthanasia.   **4**   **KU**

(b) Explain how the UK Law on euthanasia could apply in John's case.   **6**   **2KU 4AE**

(c) How helpful would the BMA guidelines on euthanasia be in this case?   **5**   **2KU 3AE**

(d) (i) What is meant by the term "sanctity of life"?

    (ii) *"Safeguarding the sanctity of life is more important than preserving the quality of life."*

    Discuss the religious and moral implications of this statement.   **15**   **3KU 12AE**

(30)

[Turn over

Question 5 – War and Peace

Marks   Code

Reminder: *You should answer this question if you have studied* **War and Peace** *in the Morality in the Modern World Unit.*

Instructions: Read the following Case Study then answer **all** parts of the question **(a) – (e)**. The number of marks available for each part of the question is indicated. You should use this as a guide to the amount of detail you should give in your answer.

Case Study

A young man, who describes himself as a conscientious objector, has refused to serve in the armed forces. He says, "I am not religious, I am objecting on moral grounds—besides which my country has made no attempt to avoid war by negotiation."

(*a*)   State **two** consequences this young man might face in his community because of his refusal to serve in the armed forces.

2   **KU**

(*b*)   Describe the role of negotiation as a response to aggression.

3   **KU**

(*c*)   What "moral grounds" might this young man have for his refusal to serve?

4   **AE**

(*d*)   How successful has the United Nations Charter been in limiting the harmful effects of war?

6   **2KU**
   4AE

(*e*)   *"We have a duty to defend our nation, if it is attacked."*

   (i)   Describe **two** religious responses to this view.

   (ii) How effectively can religious people defend this view?

15   **4KU**
   11AE

(30)

[END OF SECTION 1]

SECTION 2

Marks   Code

Christianity: Belief and Science

Instructions: Read the following extract then answer **all** parts of the question *(a) – (g)*. The number of marks available for each question is indicated. You should use these as a guide to the amount of detail you should give in your answer.

Extract

Modern science says that we inhabit a small planet in a solar system near the edge of one galaxy of stars which is only one of many millions of galaxies. The planet has existed for about five billion years and human life evolved from simpler forms of life before emerging around two million years ago. When our planet eventually dies it will not be an event of any importance to the universe which will go on existing for billions more years.

(a) What evidence might science put forward to support evolutionary theory?   **5   KU**

(b) The extract suggests that humans are insignificant. Describe Christian views on the importance of humans in the universe.   **5   KU**

(c) In what ways does the scientific method differ from revelation?   **4   KU**

(d) What are the main points of Paley's design argument?   **4   KU**

(e) Why do some Christians insist on a literal understanding of the Genesis creation stories?   **6   AE**

(f) What objections do some Christians raise against a literal understanding of the Genesis creation stories?   **6   AE**

(g) *"Revelation and evolutionary theory both contribute to a full understanding of the origins of human life."*

  Explain how scientists might respond to this statement.   **10   3KU**
                                                                                       7AE

                                                                                   (40)

[END OF SECTION 2]

[END OF QUESTION PAPER]

[BLANK PAGE]

X213/302

NATIONAL QUALIFICATIONS 2007	FRIDAY, 25 MAY 3.05 PM – 4.00 PM	**RELIGIOUS, MORAL AND PHILOSOPHICAL STUDIES** HIGHER Paper 2

You should answer **either**

Section 1:   Buddhism

or

Section 2:   Christianity

or

Section 3:   Hinduism

or

Section 4:   Islam

or

Section 5:   Judaism

or

Section 6:   Sikhism

The skills of knowledge and understanding (KU) and analysis and evaluation (AE) are being assessed in this paper. When answering each question you should note the number of marks allocated to each skill as indicated after each part of the question.

SCOTTISH QUALIFICATIONS AUTHORITY
©

Section 1 – Buddhism   *Marks   Code*

Reminder: *You should choose this section if you have studied* **Buddhism** *in the World Religion Unit. Answer* **BOTH** *questions (1 and 2) in this section of the paper.*

Question 1

Instructions: *Read the following source then answer* **all** *parts of Question 1 (a) – (f). The number of marks available for each part is indicated. Use these as a guide to the amount of detail you should include in your answer.*

Source

Look at these grey-white dried bones, like dried empty gourds thrown away at the end of the summer. Who will feel joy in looking at them?
A house of bones is this body, bones covered with flesh and with blood. Pride and hypocrisy dwell in this house and also old age and death.
. . .Those who in their youth did not live in self-harmony, and who did not gain the true treasures of life, are later like broken bows, ever deploring old things past and gone.

Dhammapada 149-150, 156

(a) *"Dried empty gourds thrown away."*

This is an example of anicca, one of the 3 Marks of Existence. Give a full description of what Buddhists understand by anicca.   **4   KU**

(b) Briefly describe the other **two** marks of existence.   **4   KU**

(c) What do Buddhists understand by samsara?   **4   KU**

(d) Explain the consequences for Buddhists of not accepting anicca.   **4   AE**

(e) What might a Buddhist understand by *"the true treasures of life"*?   **2   KU**
                                                                           2   AE
(f) Explain the relationship between anatta and samsara.   **5   AE**

                                                                           (25)

Question 2   *Marks   Code*

Instructions: Read the **statement** below then answer the *question* that follows.

Statement:

"Some people claim that Buddhism is a selfish religion because it concentrates on individual enlightenment."

Discuss **two** possible Buddhist responses to this claim.   **15   5KU**
                                                                                        10AE

                                                                                        (15)

                                                                                        (40)

                                                                          [Turn over

Section 2 – Christianity   *Marks*   *Code*

Reminder: *You should choose this section if you have studied* **Christianity** *in the World Religion Unit. Answer* **BOTH** *questions (**1** and **2**) in this section of the paper.*

Question 1

Instructions: *Read the following source then answer* **all** *parts of Question 1 (**a**) – (**e**). The number of marks available for each part is indicated. Use these as a guide to the amount of detail you should include in your answer.*

Source

Peter said to them, "Each one of you must turn away from his sins and be baptised in the name of Jesus Christ, so that your sins will be forgiven; and you will receive God's gift, the Holy Spirit".

Acts 2:38

(a) According to Genesis how did sin come into the world?	3	**KU**
(b) What is meant by *"you will receive God's gift, the Holy Spirit"*?	3	**KU**
(c) Explain why Christians think it is important to follow the teachings of Jesus.	6	**3KU 3AE**
(d) Explain what Christians understand by turning away from sin.	6	**2KU 4AE**
(e) Explain the importance of worship in building God's Kingdom on Earth.	7	**3KU 4AE**
	(25)	

Question 2

Instructions: Read the **statement** below then answer the **question** that follows.

Statement:

"Human beings are called to account for their actions after death."

With reference to **two** traditions you have studied discuss the importance for Christians of belief in judgement.   15   **5KU 10AE**

(15)

(40)

Section 3 – Hinduism   *Marks   Code*

Reminder: *You should choose this section if you have studied* **Hinduism** *in the World Religion Unit. Answer* **BOTH** *questions (*1 *and* 2*) in this section of the paper.*

Question 1

Instructions: *Read the following source then answer* **all** *parts of Question 1 (a) – (e). The number of marks available for each part is indicated. Use these as a guide to the amount of detail you should include in your answer.*

Source

The bliss that the stainless consciousness, washed by concentration
May have when it has been brought into the self
Cannot be described by speech:
It is experienced directly through the inner organ

Water in water, fire in fire
Or space in space cannot be made out:
Just so the one whose mind has gone within
Is completely freed.

                                                            Maitri Upanishad 4 v 6

(a) *"Just so the one whose mind has gone within
     Is completely freed."*

     Explain what Hindus believe about samadhi.   3   **KU**

(b) What are the key features of meditation?   3   **KU**

(c) Why is release from samsara considered desirable by Hindus?   4   **KU**

(d) Explain some of the problems associated with the attainment of moksha. 7   **3KU
                                                                                 4AE**

(e) Why is the performance of dharma so important to Hindus?   8   **2KU
                                                                                 6AE**

                                                                           (25)

Question 2

Assess the importance of ahimsa in Hinduism.   15   **5KU
                                                                                 10AE**

                                                                           (15)

                                                                           (40)

                                                            [Turn over

Section 4 – Islam   *Marks   Code*

Reminder: *You should choose this section if you have studied* **Islam** *in the World Religion Unit. Answer* **BOTH** *questions (***1*** and ***2***) in this section of the paper.*

Question 1

Instructions: *Read the following source then answer* **all** *parts of Question 1 (a) – (e). The number of marks available for each part is indicated. Use these as a guide to the amount of detail you should include in your answer.*

Source

It is not righteousness that ye turn your faces towards East or West; But it is righteousness—To believe in God and the Last Day, and the Angels and the Book and the Messengers; To spend of your substance, out of love for Him, For your kin, For orphans, For the needy, For the wayfarer, For those who ask, And for the ransom of slaves; To be steadfast in prayer, And practice regular charity; To fulfil the contracts which ye have made: And to be firm and patient in pain (or suffering) And adversity; And throughout All periods of panic. Such are the people of truth, the God–fearing.

Sura 2 v 177

(a) *"To believe in . . . the Messengers."*

   Who are the "Messengers" referred to in the passage?   3   KU

(b) Why is "the Book" important to Muslims?   3   KU

(c) *"To be steadfast in prayer,"*

   Discuss the importance of prayer for Muslims.   4   2KU
                                                                                     2AE

(d) *". . . be firm and patient in pain (or suffering) And adversity."*

   In what ways does this command benefit Muslims?   7   3KU
                                                                                     4AE

(e) Explain the significance for Muslims of belief in the day of judgement.   8   4KU
                                                                                     4AE

                                                                                    (25)

Question 2

Marks   Code

Instructions: Read the **statement** below then answer the *question* that follows.

Statement:

"The problems caused by the human condition can be overcome through the practice of Hajj."

To what extent would Muslims agree with this statement.

15   5KU
10AE

(15)

(40)

[Turn over

Section 5 – Judaism

Marks   *Code*

Reminder: *You should choose this section if you have studied **Judaism** in the World Religion Unit. Answer **BOTH** questions (**1** and **2**) in this section of the paper.*

Question 1

Instructions: *Read the following source then answer **all** parts of Question 1 (a) – (e). The number of marks available for each part is indicated. Use these as a guide to the amount of detail you should include in your answer.*

Source

And God created man in His own image, in the image of God created He him; male and female created He them.

Genesis 1:27

And the LORD God called unto the man, and said unto him: 'Where are thou?' And he said: 'I heard Thy voice in the garden, and I was afraid, because I was naked; and I hid myself. 'And He said: 'Who told thee that thou wast naked? Hast thou eaten of the tree, whereof I commanded thee that thou shouldest not eat?' And the man said: 'The woman whom Thou gavest to be with me, she gave me of the tree, and I did eat. 'And the LORD God said unto the woman: 'What is this thou hast done?' And the woman said: 'The serpent beguiled me, and I did eat.'

Genesis 3: 9-13

(a) What do Jews mean when they say man is made "in the image of God"?   **4**   **KU**

(b) How were the man, the woman and the serpent each punished as a result of their actions?   **3**   **KU**

(c) Explain Jewish beliefs about the Yetzer Tov and the Yetzer Harah.   **5**   **2KU** **3AE**

(d) Explain the importance of the principles of repentance and forgiveness in Judaism.   **6**   **2KU** **4AE**

(e) Assess the role of the prophets as the social and moral conscience of the Jewish people.   **7**   **3KU** **4AE**

(25)

Question 2

Marks   Code

Instructions: Read the **statement** below then answer the **question** that follows.

Statement:

"The responsibilities of Judaism are essential in maintaining the religious identity of both family and community."

Discuss Jewish responses to this view.

15   **5KU**
       10AE

(15)

(40)

[Turn over

Section 6 – Sikhism

Marks   Code

Reminder: *You should choose this section if you have studied* **Sikhism** *in the World Religion Unit. Answer* **BOTH** *questions (1 and 2) in this section of the paper.*

Question 1

Instructions: *Read the following source then answer* **all** *parts of Question 1 (a) – (f). The number of marks available for each part is indicated. Use these as a guide to the amount of detail you should include in your answer.*

Source

Mortals are known by their actions; this is the way it has to be. They should show goodness, and not be deformed by their actions . . .

One who walks in harmony with the Will of the True Guru, is blended with the Lord. The Messenger of Death cannot even see him; his heart is illumined with God's light . . . he does not rot away in the womb of reincarnation ever again . . .

Guru Granth Sahib, 1245

(a) What would a Sikh understand by the phrase '*True Guru*'?   **2   KU**

(b) Describe Sikh beliefs about God's Will.   **3   KU**

(c) What do Sikhs believe about the Ten Gurus?   **3   KU**

(d) Explain why the Guru Granth Sahib is called the Living Guru.   **4   2KU**
2AE

(e) Explain the phrase '*the womb of reincarnation.*'   **5   1KU**
4AE

(f) In what ways do sewa and simran help Sikhs to walk '*in harmony with the Will of the True Guru*'?   **8   4KU**
4AE

(25)

Question 2

Marks   Code

Instructions: Read the **statement** below then answer the *question* that follows.

Statement:

"It is not possible for human beings to be completely free from the powerful influences of maya and haumai."

Discuss **two** possible Sikh responses to this statement.

15   **5KU**
     10AE

(15)

(40)

[END OF QUESTION PAPER]

[BLANK PAGE]

[BLANK PAGE]

[RMPS/SQP261]

Religious, Moral and Philosophical Studies Higher Paper 1 Specimen Question Paper	Time: 1 hours 45 mins	NATIONAL QUALIFICATIONS

There are two Sections in this paper:

Section 1 – Morality in the Modern World
Section 2 – Christianity: Belief and Science

You should answer **two** questions from Section 1: Question 1 and **one** from **either**
Question 2 – Gender **or**
Question 3 – Crime and Punishment **or**
Question 4 – Medical Ethics **or**
Question 5 – War and Peace.

Section 2 has **one** mandatory question.

The skills of knowledge and understanding (KU) and analysis and evaluation (AE) are being assessed in this paper. When answering each question you should note the number of marks allocated to each skill as indicated after each part of the question.

SCOTTISH
QUALIFICATIONS
AUTHORITY

©

SECTION 1

Marks   Code

Morality in the Modern World

You **must** answer **Question 1 (a) and (b)** and **one** other question (**either** 2 **or** 3 **or** 4 **or** 5)

Question 1

Instructions: Read the following extract then answer **both** parts of the question **(a) and (b)**. The number of marks for each part is indicated. You should use these as a guide to the amount of detail you should include in your answer.

> *Extract:*
>
> **Socrates:**   And what do you say of piety, . . . is not piety, according to your definition, loved by all the gods?
>
> **Euthyphro:** Yes
>
> **Socrates:**   Because it is pious or holy, or for some other reason?

(a) What issue is raised by the Euthyphro dilemma?   **4   KU**

(b) Describe **three** sources of moral guidance which are found in **one** or **more** religious traditions.   **6   KU**

(10)

Page two

Question 2 – Gender   *Marks   Code*

Reminder: *You should answer this question if you have studied **Gender Issues** in the Morality in the Modern World Unit.*

Instructions: Read the statement below then answer **all** parts of the question **(a) – (d)**. The number of marks available for each part of the question is indicated. You should use this as a guide to the amount of detail you should include in your answer.

Statement:

"The stereotyping of women promotes disrespect. It treats women as objects to be exploited and manipulated. Furthermore, it degrades the role and status of women in society."

(a) Describe ways in which women are stereotyped.   **5**   **KU**

(b) What evidence might be offered to suport the claim that religion "degrades the role and status of women in society"?   **5**   **KU**

(c) To what extent has society been successful in combating gender stereotyping?   **5**   **AE**

(d) "Society is now the force that shapes male and female roles."

Discuss the religious and moral implications of this statement.   **15**   **AE**

                                                                                  (30)

Question 3 – Crime and Punishment

Marks Code

Reminder: *You should answer this question if you have studied* **Crime and Punishment** *in the Morality in the Modern World Unit.*

Instructions: Read the following Case Study then answer **all** parts of the question *(a) – (d)*. The number of marks available for each part of the question is indicated. You should use this as a guide to the amount of detail you should give in your answer.

Case Study

David awoke and his immediate thought was how to get his first fix. This would take him to midday. Without this, the torment would soon begin, and continue until he had managed to inject. His first priority was, therefore, to get the money for this one fix; the rest he could take care of later. A visit to the local supermarket would enable him to steal a few packets of bacon and cheese, easy to sell in the local bar. As he left the supermarket bypassing the waiting line of customers prepared to pay for their purchases he was stopped by the store manager. "Sir would you accompany me back to my office."

The familiar run of events followed, ending with him standing before a judge pleading guilty to theft.

In his plea of mitigation he said, "I need to steal, your honour. I have a drug habit that I need to feed."

The judge decided to send David to prison.

(a) Describe **three** purposes of punishment.   **6**   KU

(b) "The judge decided to send David to prison."

Explain possible benefits and drawbacks of this sentence.   **6**   AE

(c) Describe **two** other forms of punishment available in the UK.   **4**   KU

(d) *"Reform is the only morally acceptable reason for punishment."*

Discuss this statement. You should include **two** different viewpoints as part of your discussion. **One** of these must be religious.   **14**   AE

(30)

Question 4 – Medical Ethics

Marks   Code

Reminder: *You should answer this question if you have studied **Medical Ethics** in the Morality in the Modern World Unit.*

Instructions: Read the following Case Study then answer **all** parts of the question **(a) – (d)**. The number of marks available for each part of the question is indicated. You should use this as a guide to the amount of detail you should give in your answer.

Case Study

Euthanasia is a difficult moral issue with no easy answers as the following example suggests:

Paul is 30 years old. Until a few years ago he lived an active and enjoyable life. He had a good job, a young and growing family and a beautiful wife. That all changed when he had his car accident.

He is now almost totally paralysed and is kept alive by sophisticated life-support machinery. His brain was not damaged in the accident and he can still speak. However, he wishes that his brain **had** been damaged because then his doctor might turn all the machines off and allow him to die in peace.

Every day he tries to persuade his doctor to turn off the machines. But she will not agree to do this.

"My work is to help save lives, Paul," she says, "not to help to end them."

(a)   Describe the law in The Netherlands in relation to euthanasia.   **4   KU**

(b)   Explain why some people may believe that euthanasia is morally wrong.   **5   2KU**
3AE

(c)   In what ways might the BMA's guidelines on euthanasia help Paul's doctor in this situation?   **6   2KU**
4AE

(d)   *"Life ultimately belongs to the individual therefore the individual alone should make decisions about ending it."*

Discuss the religious and moral implications of this statement.   **15   3KU**
12AE

(30)

Question 5 – War and Peace   *Marks   Code*

Reminder: *You should answer this question if you have studied **War and Peace** in the Morality in the Modern World Unit.*

Instructions: Read the following information then answer **all** parts of the question *(a) – (e)*. The number of marks available for each part of the question is indicated. You should use this as a guide to the amount of detail you should give in your answer.

Information

It is claimed that the first weapons of mass destruction (WMD) were gas attacks launched by the German army from the trenches around Ypres in 1915. Since 1945 the threat from weapons of mass destruction has significantly increased. The need for international monitoring of WMD has never been greater.

(a) Describe **three** modern weapons of mass destruction.   **3   KU**

(b) Explain the ways in which WMD differ from conventional weapons.   **3   KU**

(c) Describe a viewpoint on the use of WMD which is independent of religious belief.   **4   KU**

(d) How effective have international conventions been in controlling WMD?   **5   AE**

(e) *"The possession of WMD is incompatible with religious teachings."*

Discuss.   **15   AE**

                    (30)

[END OF SECTION 1]

SECTION 2

Marks   Code

Christianity: Belief and Science

Instructions: Read the following extract then answer **all** parts of the question **(a) – (g)**. The number of marks available for each question is indicated. You should use these as a guide to the amount of detail you should give in your answer.

Extract:

Some Christians reject the Big Bang theory because it seems to contradict the belief that God created the Universe. This belief is based on the account of the creation of the Universe in Genesis.

Scientists follow a systematic method when developing and testing their theories. However, Christians do not use one systematic method to arrive at their beliefs. In general they may use a number of sources including:

- revelation
- reasoned argument based on observation of the world.

The second of these is closest to scientific method but there is an important difference: most scientists have little difficulty modifying their theories when the need arises but some Christians find it difficult to modify their beliefs.

(a) Describe the Cosmological Argument.   **5   KU**

(b) Describe scientific method.   **6   KU**

(c) Explain **two** ways in which scientific method is said to be limited.   **4   AE**

(d) Describe what is meant by revelation in the Christian tradition.   **5   KU**

(e) Give **two** reasons why someone might believe that scientific method is a more reliable source of knowledge than Christian revelation.   **4   AE**

(f) Why do some Christians insist on a literal interpretation of Genesis 1?   **6   2KU
                                                                               4AE**

(g) *"It is perfectly reasonable for Christians to believe in a Creator God and to accept Big Bang theory."*

   Do you agree? Give reasons for your answer.   **10   3KU
                                                                               7AE**

[*END OF SECTION 2*]

                                                                          (40)

[*END OF SPECIMEN QUESTION PAPER*]

[BLANK PAGE]

[RMPS/SQP261]

Religious, Moral and Philosophical Studies Higher Paper 2 Specimen Question Paper	Time: 55 mins	NATIONAL QUALIFICATIONS

You should answer **either**

Section 1:   Buddhism

or

Section 2:   Christianity

or

Section 3:   Hinduism

or

Section 4:   Islam

or

Section 5:   Judaism

or

Section 6:   Sikhism

The skills of knowledge and understanding (KU) and analysis and evaluation (AE) are being assessed in this paper. When answering each question you should note the number of marks allocated to each skill as indicated after each part of the question.

SCOTTISH QUALIFICATIONS AUTHORITY

Section 1 – Buddhism   *Marks   Code*

Reminder: *You should choose this section if you have studied **Buddhism** in the World Religion Unit. Answer **BOTH** questions (**1** and **2**) in this section of the paper.*

Question 1

Instructions: *Read the following source then answer **all** parts of Question 1 (**a**)–(**f**). The number of marks available for each part is indicated. Use these as a guide to the amount of detail you should include in your answer.*

Source

Consider this body! A painted puppet with jointed limbs, sometimes suffering and covered with ulcers, full of imaginings, never permanent, for ever changing.

This body is decaying! A nest of diseases, a heap of corruption, bound to destruction, to dissolution. All life ends in death.

....

I have gone round in vain the cycles of many lives ever striving to find the builder of the house of life and death. How great is the sorrow of life that must die!
But now I have seen thee, housebuilder: never more shalt thou build this house. The rafters of sin are broken, the ridge-pole of ignorance is destroyed. The fever of craving is past: for my mortal mind is gone to the immortal Nirvana.

Dhammapada 147-8, 153-4

(a) *This source helps to explain anatta, one of the 3 Marks of Existence.*

Describe the other **two** Marks of Existence.   **2   KU**

(b) *"Consider this body! . . . full of imaginings, never permanent, for ever changing."*

Describe each of the "5 skandhas".   **5   KU**

(c) *"I have gone round in vain the cycles of many lives."*

Describe what Buddhists understand by samsara.   **4   KU**

(d) Explain how attachment to the self leads to the rebuilding of "the house of life and death".   **6   AE**

	Marks	Code

Question 1 (continued)

(*e*) How successful is anatta alone in helping to explain the Human Condition?

4   **AE**

(*f*) Explain what Buddhists understand by "the fever of craving".

4   **1KU**
     3AE

(25)

Question 2

Instructions: Read the **statement** below then answer the *question* that follows.

Statement:

"*Without meditation we cannot achieve enlightenment.*"

Discuss **two** possible Buddhist responses to this statement.

15   **7KU**
     8AE

(15)

(40)

Section 2 – Christianity

Marks   *Code*

Reminder: *You should choose this section if you have studied* **Christianity** *in the World Religion Unit. Answer* **BOTH** *questions (1 and 2) in this section of the paper.*

Question 1

Instructions: *Read the following source then answer* **all** *parts of Question 1 (a)–(e). The number of marks available for each part is indicated. Use these as a guide to the amount of detail you should include in your answer.*

Source

When the Son of Man comes as King and all the angels with him, he will sit on his royal throne, and the people of all the nations will be gathered before him. Then he will divide them into two groups, just as the shepherd separates the sheep from the goats. He will put the righteous people on his right and the others on his left. Then the King will say to the people on his right, "Come you that are blessed by my Father!" Come and possess the kingdom which has been prepared for ever since the creation of the world.

Matt 25: 31 -34

(a) What do Christians understand by the "Son of Man"?   **4**   **KU**

(b) *"Come you that are blessed by my Father!"*

What did Jesus teach about how this state of being blessed can be achieved?   **4**   **KU**

(c) Explain the role of worship in building the Kingdom of God.   **6**   **2KU**
    4AE

(d) Explain what Christians understand by *Eternal Life*.   **8**   **4KU**
    4AE

(e) What do Christians mean when they describe Jesus as a *King*?   **3**   **AE**

(25)

Question 2

Instructions: Read the **statement** below then answer the **question** that follows.

Statement:

"Without belief in the Resurrection of Jesus the Christian faith is pointless."

Discuss this statement with reference to **two** different Christian responses.   **15**   **5KU**
    10AE

(15)

(40)

Section 3 – Hinduism

Marks Code

Reminder: *You should choose this section if you have studied* **Hinduism** *in the World Religion Unit. Answer* **BOTH** *questions (1 and 2) in this section of the paper.*

Question 1

Instructions: *Read the following source then answer* **all** *parts of Question 1 (a)–(e). The number of marks available for each part is indicated. Use these as a guide to the amount of detail you should include in your answer.*

Source

Living in the midst of ignorance,
Wise in their own view, thinking themselves learned,
The foolish roam about,
Like blind men led by one who is blind.

Mundaka Upanishad

(a) What is the "ignorance" to which the passage refers?   3   **KU**

(b) Why are the "foolish" considered to be "like blind men led by one who is blind"?   3   **KU**

(c) Explain the role of avidya in the human condition.   8   **4KU**
4AE

(d) *"Greater is thine own work, even if this be humble, than the work of another, even if this be great."*

Bhagavad Gita

What does this extract tell Hindus about dharma?   6   **KU**

(e) How far do Hindus agree on the nature of the atman?   5   **1KU**
4AE

Question 2   (25)

Instructions: Read the **statement** below then answer the *question* that follows.

Statement:

"In practising the margas Hindus have to reject the world and all that is in it."

Would Hindus agree with this statement? Discuss.   15   **4KU**
11AE

(15)

(40)

Section 4 – Islam

Marks   Code

Reminder: *You should choose this section if you have studied* **Islam** *in the World Religion Unit. Answer* **BOTH** *questions (1 and 2) in this section of the paper.*

Question 1

Instructions: *Read the following source then answer* **all** *parts of Question 1 (a)–(e). The number of marks available for each part is indicated. Use these as a guide to the amount of detail you should include in your answer.*

Source

But Satan whispered evil to him: he said, "O Adam! shall I lead thee to the Tree of Eternity and to a kingdom that never decays?" In the result, they both ate of the tree, and so their nakedness appeared to them: they began to sew together, for their covering, leaves from the Garden: thus did Adam disobey his Lord, and allow himself to be seduced. But his Lord chose him (for his Grace): He turned to him, and gave him Guidance.

He said: "Get ye down, both of you,—all together from the Garden, with enmity one to another: but if, as is sure, there comes to you Guidance from Me, whosoever follows My Guidance, will not lose his way, nor fall into misery.
"But whosoever turned away from My Message, verily for him is a life narrowed down, and We shall raise him up blind on the Day of Judgement." He will say: "O my Lord! why hast Thou raised me up blind, while I had sight (before)?

(God) will say: "Thus didst Thou, when Our Signs came unto thee, disregard them: so wilt thou, this day, be disregarded".

Surah 20

(a) "In the result, they both ate of the tree."

Describe Muslim beliefs about the consequences of this action.   **3   KU**

(b) Describe the concept of freewill as understood by Muslims.   **3   KU**

(c) Explain what Muslims understand to be the purpose of suffering in the present life.   **7   3KU**
4AE

(d) Explain Muslim beliefs about The Day of Judgement.   **7   5KU**
2AE

Question 1 (continued)   *Marks*   *Code*

    (e) *"There comes to you Guidance from Me, whosoever follows My Guidance, will not lose his way, nor fall into misery."*

        Explain the significance of Guidance for Muslims.   **5**   **2KU**
                                                                         3AE

Question 2   **(25)**

Instructions: Read the **statement** below then answer the ***question*** that follows.

Statement:

"The observance of zakat makes the biggest contribution to helping Muslims overcome the problems of the human condition."

Discuss.   **15**   **4KU**
                                                                         11AE

                                                                         (15)

                                                                         (40)

Section 5 – Judaism   *Marks   Code*

Reminder: *You should choose this section if you have studied* **Judaism** *in the World Religion Unit. Answer* **BOTH** *questions (1 and 2) in this section of the paper.*

Question 1

Instructions: *Read the following source then answer* **all** *parts of Question 1 (a)–(e). The number of marks available for each part is indicated. Use these as a guide to the amount of detail you should include in your answer.*

Source

(Know that) I am the Lord thy God who brought thee out of the land of Egypt

Thou shalt have no other gods before me

Thou shalt not take the name of the Lord thy God in vain

Remember the Sabbath day to keep it holy

Honour thy father and thy mother

Thou shalt not commit adultery

Thou shalt not steal

Thou shalt not bear false witness against thy neighbour

Thou shalt not covet thy neighbour's house.   Thou shalt not covet thy neighbour's wife, nor his man-servant, nor his maid-servant, . . . nor anything that is thy neighbour's

Exodus 20: 2-14

(a) Describe the event being referred to in the first two lines of this source.   **2**   **KU**

(b) Explain why the Covenant made with Moses is important to Jews.   **4**   **2KU**
                                                                                2AE

(c) Describe the ways in which Jews show that the Sabbath is a day dedicated to God.   **6**   **KU**

(d) *"Thou shalt not bear false witness against thy neighbour."*

   Explain Jewish beliefs regarding the treatment of one's "neighbour".   **6**   **2KU**
                                                                              4AE

(e) How difficult is it for Jews today to obey God's laws? You should refer to **three** different laws **other** than Sabbath laws in your answer.   **7**   **3KU**
                                                                                          4AE

                                                                                    (25)

Question 2

Marks   Code

Instructions: Read the **statement** below then answer the *question* that follows.

Statement:

"Evil and suffering result when human beings ignore God's guidance and misuse the gift of freewill."

How successfully does Judaism explain the existence of evil and suffering?

Give reasons for your answer.

15   5KU
10AE

(15)

(40)

Section 6 – Sikhism

Marks   *Code*

Reminder: *You should choose this section if you have studied* **Sikhism** *in the World Religion Unit. Answer* **BOTH** *questions (1 and 2) in this section of the paper.*

Question 1

Instructions: *Read the following source then answer* **all** *parts of Question 1 (a)–(e). The number of marks available for each part is indicated. Use these as a guide to the amount of detail you should include in your answer.*

Source

The foolish self-willed manmukh does not remember the Lord's Name; he wastes away his life in vain. But when he meets the True Guru, then obtains the Name; he sheds egotism and emotional attachment.

. . . Within this body dwell the five (evils): . . . They plunder the Nectar, but the self-willed manmukh does not realise it; no one hears his complaint . . . But one who becomes Gurmukh meditates on the Naam, and ever contemplates the Lord's Name. Through The True Word of Gurbani, he sings the Glorious praises of the Lord; blessed with the Lord's glance of Grace, he is enraptured . . . Serving the Perfect Guru, (he) becomes carefree, enshrining the Lord within the heart; doubt is eradicated from within.

Guru Granth Sahib, 600

(a) What would a Sikh understand by the phrase "True Guru"?   **2**   **KU**

(b) Describe each of the five evils mentioned in the second paragraph of the source.   **5**   **KU**

(c) What is the importance of practicing Nam Simran for Sikhs?   **4**   **2KU 2AE**

(d) Explain why, according to the Sikh faith, the "foolish self-willed manmukh . . . wastes away his life in vain".   **6**   **2KU 4AE**

(e) Explain Sikh beliefs about the final goal of human life.   **8**   **4KU 4AE**

(25)

Page ten

Question 2   *Marks   Code*

Instructions: Read the **statement** below then answer the *question* that follows.

Statement:

"*The belief that all people are equal is a very difficult belief to put into practice.*"

Discuss **two** possible Sikh responses to this statement.   15   **5KU**
                                                                                  10AE

                                                                                 (15)

                                                                                 (40)

[*END OF SPECIMEN QUESTION PAPER*]

[BLANK PAGE]

[BLANK PAGE]

X213/301

NATIONAL
QUALIFICATIONS
2008

WEDNESDAY, 28 MAY
1.00 PM – 2.45 PM

RELIGIOUS, MORAL
AND PHILOSOPHICAL
STUDIES
HIGHER
Paper 1

There are two Sections in this paper:

Section 1 – Morality in the Modern World
Section 2 – Christianity: Belief and Science

You should answer **two** questions from Section 1: Question 1 and **one** from **either**

Question 2 – Gender **or**
Question 3 – Crime and Punishment **or**
Question 4 – Medical Ethics **or**
Question 5 – War and Peace.

Section 2 has **one** mandatory question.

The skills of knowledge and understanding (KU) and analysis and evaluation (AE) are being assessed in this paper. When answering each question you should note the number of marks allocated to each skill as indicated after each part of the question.

SECTION 1

Marks   Code

Morality in the Modern World

You **must** answer **Question 1 (*a*) – (*c*)** and **one** other question (**either** 2 **or** 3 **or** 4 **or** 5)

Question 1

Instructions: Answer **all** parts of the question (*a*) – (*c*). The number of marks available can be found at the end of each question. You should use these as a guide to the amount of detail you should include in your answer.

(*a*) Describe **one** way in which sacred writings guide moral values in one religion you have studied.

2   **KU**

(*b*) Explain the role of duty and reason in moral decision making.

4   **KU**

(*c*) What are the key features of consequentialist ethics?

4   **KU**

(10)

Question 2 – Gender

Marks   Code

Reminder: *You should answer this question if you have studied **Gender Issues** in the Morality in the Modern World Unit.*

Instructions: Read the following extract then answer **all** parts of the question **(a) – (e)**. The number of marks available for each part of the question is indicated. You should use this as a guide to the amount of detail you should include in your answer.

Extract

"It is a startling fact that the majority of the world's poor are women and girls. We can argue about the reasons behind this but one thing is clear—economic equality between men and women is an essential step towards a more just world."

(a) What does UK law say about equal pay?

2   KU

(b) *"Equal pay in the UK is not yet a reality."*

Do you agree?

6   2KU
4AE

(c) How might UN declarations make a difference to the economic relationship between men and women?

4   2KU
2AE

(d) *"The pursuit of economic equality is not in women's interests."*

Why might some religious people agree?

6   AE

(e) *"Economic equality between men and women is an essential step towards a more just world."*

Discuss with reference to at least **one** viewpoint independent of religious belief.

12   4KU
8AE

(30)

[Turn over

Question 3 – Crime and Punishment

Marks   Code

Reminder: *You should answer this question if you have studied* **Crime and Punishment** *in the Morality in the Modern World Unit.*

Instructions: Read the following extract then answer **all** parts of the question **(a) – (e)**.   The number of marks available for each part of the question is indicated.   You should use this as a guide to the amount of detail you should include in your answer.

> ### Extract
>
> "Two fishermen who raped and murdered a student in Thailand, were sentenced to death.   They will be executed by lethal injection."

(a)   State **two** arguments that can be used to support capital punishment.   2   **KU**

(b)   Describe what the United Nations says about capital punishment.   2   **KU**

(c)   *"Some forms of execution are more morally justifiable than others."*

Do you agree?   6   **2KU**
4AE

(d)   Explain why the case of Timothy Evans was a significant factor in abolishing capital punishment in the UK.   6   **2KU**
4AE

(e)   *"Capital punishment is an acceptable form of punishment."*

Discuss this statement with reference to two different viewpoints found within religion.   14   **2KU**
12AE

(30)

Question 4 – Medical Ethics   *Marks   Code*

Reminder: *You should answer this question if you have studied **Medical Ethics** in the Morality in the Modern World Unit.*

Instructions: Read the following extract then answer **all** parts of the question **(a) – (e)**. The number of marks available for each part of the question is indicated. You should use this as a guide to the amount of detail you should include in your answer.

Extract

The HFEA has permitted research on embryos for genetic engineering. In time the aim of genetic engineering is to treat and prevent hereditary diseases and disorders. However, human cloning for reproductive purposes is against the law.

(a) Describe what is meant by "genetic engineering".   **2**   **KU**

(b) What are the HFEA guidelines on the use of human embryos in research?   **4**   **KU**

(c) What concerns might there be about the use of human embryos in research?   **4**   **AE**

(d) "... the aim of genetic engineering is to treat and prevent hereditary diseases and disorders."

Why might some religious people support this aim?   **5**   **AE**

(e) "Human cloning for reproductive purposes can never be right."

Do you agree with this statement? Give reasons for your answer.   **15** **3KU**
                                                                         12AE

                                                                   (30)

[Turn over

Question 5 – War and Peace   *Marks   Code*

Reminder: *You should answer this question if you have studied **War and Peace** in the Morality in the Modern World Unit.*

Instructions: Read the following extract then answer **all** parts of the question *(a)* – *(e)*. The number of marks available for each part of the question is indicated. You should use this as a guide to the amount of detail you should include in your answer.

Extract

"In many religions there are groups who refuse to fight in a war for any reason."

(a) What is pacifism?   **2   KU**

(b) What does the UN Charter say about War?   **3   KU**

(c) Describe the arguments in favour of pacifism from a viewpoint independent of religion.   **4   KU**

(d) Why might religious people disagree about whether it is morally right to go to war?   **6   AE**

(e) *"Pacifism is no longer a realistic stance."*

Discuss the religious and moral implications of this statement.   **15   2KU**
                                                                         13AE

                                                                         (30)

[END OF SECTION 1]

SECTION 2

Marks   *Code*

Christianity: Belief and Science

Instructions: Read the following extract then answer **all** parts of the question **(a) – (h)**. The number of marks available for each question is indicated. You should use these as a guide to the amount of detail you should include in your answer.

Extract

"Revelation **and** the Big Bang theory both contribute to a full understanding of the origins of the universe."

(a) What evidence is used to support the Big Bang Theory?   **4**   **KU**

(b) Describe two ways in which Christians might understand the creation stories in Genesis.   **4**   **KU**

(c) Describe the key features of the cosmological argument.   **4**   **KU**

(d) In what ways is the Big Bang Theory compatible with the cosmological argument?   **4**   **AE**

(e) What reasons do some Christians have for rejecting the Big Bang Theory?   **4**   **KU**

(f) Why might some Christians consider the scientific method to be limited?   **5**   **AE**

(g) Why might some scientists reject revelation?   **5**   **AE**

(h) *"Evolutionary theory has removed the need for a designer of the universe."*

How successfully do Christians respond to this challenge?   **10**   **4KU**
     6AE

(40)

[END OF SECTION 2]

[END OF QUESTION PAPER]

[BLANK PAGE]

X213/302

NATIONAL
QUALIFICATIONS
2008

WEDNESDAY, 28 MAY
3.05 PM – 4.00 PM

RELIGIOUS, MORAL
AND PHILOSOPHICAL
STUDIES
HIGHER
Paper 2

You should answer **either**

Section 1:   Buddhism

or

Section 2:   Christianity

or

Section 3:   Hinduism

or

Section 4:   Islam

or

Section 5:   Judaism

or

Section 6:   Sikhism

The skills of knowledge and understanding (KU) and analysis and evaluation (AE) are being assessed in this paper. When answering each question you should note the number of marks allocated to each skill as indicated after each part of the question.

Section 1 – Buddhism

Marks   Code

Reminder: *You should choose this section if you have studied* **Buddhism** *in the World Religion Unit. Answer* **BOTH** *questions (***1** *and* **2***) in this section of the paper.*

Question 1

Instructions: *Read the following source then answer* **all** *parts of Question 1 (**a**) – (**f**). The number of marks available for each part is indicated. Use these as a guide to the amount of detail you should include in your answer.*

Source

Look upon the man who tells thee thy faults as if he told thee of a hidden treasure, the wise man who shows thee the dangers of life. Follow that man: he who follows him will see good and not evil.

Let him admonish and let him instruct, and let him restrain what is wrong. He will be loved by those who are good and hated by those who are not.

Have not for friends those whose soul is ugly; go not with men who have an evil soul. Have for friends those whose soul is beautiful; go with men whose soul is good.

He who drinks of the waters of Truth, he rests in joy with mind serene. The wise find their delight in the DHAMMA, in the Truth revealed by the great.

Dhammapada 76–79

(a) Describe the role of the Buddha in revealing the dhamma.   **4**   **KU**

(b) Describe what Buddhists understand by kamma.   **5**   **KU**

(c) What would Buddhists consider to be "*the dangers of life*"?   **3**   **KU**

(d) Why would knowing about your faults be considered "*a hidden treasure*"?   **2**   **AE**

(e) The dhamma is not the source of enlightenment; it only indicates the way.

    Explain why Buddhists would believe this to be the case.   **3**   **AE**

(f) Discuss the view that the Sangha is central to Buddhism.   **8**   **2KU**
                                                                                                                              6AE

(25)

Question 2

Marks Code

Instructions: Read the **statement** below then answer the *question* that follows.

Statement:

"The arhat is the true ideal of Buddhism."

Would all Buddhists agree?

15 **5KU**
10AE

(15)

(40)

[Turn over

Section 2 – Christianity

Marks   Code

Reminder: *You should choose this section if you have studied* **Christianity** *in the World Religion Unit. Answer* **BOTH** *questions (1 and 2) in this section of the paper.*

Question 1

Instructions: *Read the following source then answer* **all** *parts of Question 1 (a)–(f). The number of marks available for each part is indicated. Use these as a guide to the amount of detail you should include in your answer.*

Source

For it is clear that it is not the angels that he helps. Instead, as the scripture says, "He helps the descendants of Abraham." This means that he had to become like his brothers in every way, in order to be their faithful and merciful High Priest in his service to God, so that the people's sins would be forgiven. And now he can help those who are tempted, because he himself was tempted and suffered.

Hebrews 2:16–18

(a) Explain what is meant by '*the descendants of Abraham*'.   2   **KU**

(b) "*. . . he had to become like his brothers . . .*"

Why is it important for Christians to believe in the humanity of Jesus?   5   **2KU**
3AE

(c) What reasons do Christians give for following the example of Jesus?   4   **KU**

(d) According to Christians, what are the main causes of suffering?   4   **KU**

(e) How might prayer and meditation help Christians achieve their goals in this life?   6   **2KU**
4AE

(f) Why might the existence of suffering be a problem for Christians?   4   **AE**

(25)

Question 2

(a) Describe the suffering and death of Jesus.   5   **KU**

(b) Assess the importance of the suffering and death of Jesus as a means of salvation.   10   **AE**

(15)

(40)

Section 3 – Hinduism

Marks Code

Reminder: *You should choose this section if you have studied* **Hinduism** *in the World Religion Unit. Answer* **BOTH** *questions (1 and 2) in this section of the paper.*

Question 1

Instructions: *Read the following source then answer* **all** *parts of Question 1 (a)–(f). The number of marks available for each part is indicated. Use these as a guide to the amount of detail you should include in your answer.*

> *Source*
>
> Greater is thine own work, even if this be humble, than the work of another, even if this be great. When a man does the work God gives him, no sin can touch this man. And a man should not abandon his work, even if he cannot achieve it in full perfection; because in all work there may be imperfection even as in all fire there is smoke.
>
> *Bhagavad Gita 18*

(a) What is the importance of sruti scripture in Hinduism?   2 KU

(b) State the dharma for each ashrama.   4 KU

(c) Describe the importance of dharma in Hinduism.   4 KU

(d) What is the relationship between karma and varna?   5 KU

(e) Explain why the caste system might be criticised.   4 AE

(f) Explain how the caste system might be defended.   6 AE

(25)

Question 2

How accurate are Hindu descriptions of the human condition?   15 4KU
11AE

(15)

(40)

[Turn over

Section 4 – Islam

Marks   Code

Reminder: *You should choose this section if you have studied **Islam** in the World Religion Unit. Answer **BOTH** questions (**1** and **2**) in this section of the paper.*

Question 1

Instructions: *Read the following source then answer **all** parts of Question 1 (a)–(e). The number of marks available for each part is indicated. Use these as a guide to the amount of detail you should include in your answer.*

Source

God! There is no god but He,—the Living the Self-Subsisting, Eternal. It is He who sent down to thee (step by step), in truth, the Book, confirming what went before it; and He sent down the Law (of Moses) and the Gospel (of Jesus) before this, as a guide to mankind, and He sent down the Criterion (of judgment between right and wrong). Then those who reject Faith in the Signs of God will suffer the severest penalty, and God is Exalted in Might, Lord of Retribution. From God, verily nothing is hidden on earth or in the heavens.

"Our Lord!" (they say), "Let not our hearts deviate now after Thou hast guided us, but grant us mercy from Thine own Presence; for Thou art the Grantor of bounties without measure."

Surah 3 vv 2–5; 8

(a) "... *who sent down to thee (step by step), in truth, the Book* ..."

Describe the ways Muslims show that "the Book" is important to them.   3   **KU**

(b) Discuss the significance of Revelation for Muslims.   6   **2KU**
                                                                          4AE

(c) "*From God, verily nothing is hidden on earth or in the heavens.*"

In what ways do Muslims respond to this passage?   3   **KU**

(d) "*Then those who reject Faith in the Signs of God will suffer the severest penalty* ..."

Describe Muslim beliefs about suffering.   5   **KU**

(e) Explain how Muslims understand the day of Judgement.   8   **3KU**
                                                                          5AE

(25)

Question 2   *Marks   Code*

Instructions: Read the **statement** below then answer the *question* that follows.

Statement:

"It is within the practice of salah that Islam finds its true identity."

Discuss this statement.

                                                          15   4KU
                                                               11AE

                                                          (15)
                                                          (40)

                                                    [Turn over

Section 5 – Judaism

Marks   *Code*

Reminder: *You should choose this section if you have studied **Judaism** in the World Religion Unit. Answer **BOTH** questions (**1** and **2**) in this section of the paper.*

Question 1

Instructions: *Read the following source then answer **all** parts of Question 1 (**a**)–(**f**). The number of marks available for each part is indicated. Use these as a guide to the amount of detail you should include in your answer.*

Source

Honour thy father and thy mother, that thy days may be long upon the land which the LORD thy God giveth thee. Thou shalt not murder. Thou shalt not commit adultery. Thou shalt not steal. Thou shalt not bear false witness against thy neighbour. Thou shalt not covet thy neighbour's house; thou shalt not covet thy neighbour's wife, nor his man-servant, nor his maid-servant, nor his ox, nor his ass, nor any thing that is thy neighbour's.

And all the people perceived the thunderings, and the lightnings, and the voice of the horn, and the mountain smoking; and when the people saw it, they trembled, and stood afar off.

Exodus 20: 11–14

(*a*) What is the importance of Moses in Jewish tradition?   3   **KU**

(*b*) *"And all the people perceived the thunderings, and the lightnings . . ."*

Give examples of ways in which Jewish people believe God has interacted with humanity.   4   **KU**

(*c*) What happens at a Bar Mitzvah ceremony?   3   **KU**

(*d*) Explain how the Ten Commandments can be seen as a summary of the mitzvoth of the Torah.   5   **2KU 3AE**

(*e*) *"Honour thy father and thy mother . . ."*

Assess the importance of the family in Judaism.   4   **2KU 2AE**

(*f*) Discuss the view that evil and suffering occur as a result of disobedience to God's will.   6   **2KU 4AE**

(25)

Question 2   *Marks   Code*

Instructions: Read the **statement** below then answer the *question* that follows.

Statement:

"The world depends on three things—on Torah study, on service to God and on kind deeds."

Is this an accurate summary of Judaism?   **15   5KU**
                                                                                       10AE

                                                                                        (15)

                                                                                        (40)

                                                                       [Turn over

Section 6 – Sikhism

Marks   *Code*

Reminder: *You should choose this section if you have studied* **Sikhism** *in the World Religion Unit. Answer* **BOTH** *questions (1 and 2) in this section of the paper.*

Question 1

Instructions: *Read the following source then answer* **all** *parts of Question 1 (a)–(e). The number of marks available for each part is indicated. Use these as a guide to the amount of detail you should include in your answer.*

Source

By His Command, bodies are created; His command cannot be described.

By His Command, souls come into being; By His command glory and greatness are obtained.

By His Command, some are high and some are low; by His Written Command, pain and pleasure are obtained. Some by His Command are blessed and forgiven; others by His Command wander aimlessly for ever.

Everyone is subject to His Command. O Nanak, one who understands His Command does not speak in ego.

Guru Granth Sahib, **1**

(a) Describe Sikh belief about God.   **3**   **KU**

(b) Describe how the Guru Granth Sahib is used in worship.   **3**   **KU**

(c) How do Sikhs show compassion and selflessness?   **3**   **KU**

(d) *". . . others by His Command wander aimlessly for ever."*

How does this explain the Sikh understanding of the human condition?   **6**   **2KU 4AE**

(e) Explain how the Five Evils create a barrier to reunion.   **10**   **5KU 5AE**

(25)

Question 2

Discuss the spiritual and physical importance of the 5 Ks for a Sikh.   **15**   **5KU 10AE**

(15)

(40)

[END OF QUESTION PAPER]

[BLANK PAGE]

[BLANK PAGE]

[BLANK PAGE]

[BLANK PAGE]

[BLANK PAGE]

[BLANK PAGE]

Pocket answer section for
SQA Higher Religious, Moral and Philosophical Studies, 2006 to 2008

© 2008 Scottish Qualifications Authority/Leckie & Leckie, All Rights Reserved

Published by Leckie & Leckie Ltd, 3rd Floor, 4 Queen Street, Edinburgh EH2 1JE
tel: 0131 220 6831, fax: 0131 225 9987, enquiries@leckieandleckie.co.uk, www.leckieandleckie.co.uk

Religious, Moral and Philosophical Studies
Higher 2006 (New Arrangements) Paper 1

Section 1

1. (a) What is meant by the claim that moral values are heteronomous?
   Description may include, eg:
   - moral values are dependent on religious belief
   - religious beliefs and values provide guidance for moral decision-making
   - 'sacred writings' may provide the main guidance for the person's moral decisions
     – other sources might be faith, tradition and God-given reason
   - may be based on the belief that only religious belief/God provides an adequate reason to be moral (eventual reward and punishment)
   - contrasts with autonomy

   (b) A description of the role of reason in one or more religious traditions, eg:
   - reason may be used to interpret and understand scripture and tradition
   - reason may be used to help reinterpret scripture and tradition in new contexts
   - reason may be the main guide to help the believer to understand for her/himself the rationality of the guidance given in sacred writings (eg Buddhism)
   - human reason is one of God's gifts which helps believers to understand God's guidance and the value of acting in harmony with God's will
   - human reason may be rejected as a source of moral guidance because it is flawed or corrupted.

   (c) A description of the ideas of Aristotle, Anscombe, Macintyre for example, ie:
   - Virtue Ethics focuses on what it means to be a 'good/virtuous person' rather than what makes an individual act 'good or right'
   - reason is an important guide in determining what constitutes a virtuous person/disposition
   - general or rigid rules are regarded as unhelpful/irrelevant
   - living a 'good/virtuous' life is an end in itself rather than a way of achieving some other ultimate goal
   - virtues are human qualities which help individuals to live a 'good' life to the benefit of themselves and all society
   - virtues lie between the extremes of excess and deficiency (the Golden Mean)
   - by living virtuously, human beings fulfil their true potential
   - does not depend on religious belief but is compatible with religious belief.

2. (a)
   - Domestic role of women
   - Leadership role of men
   - Working role of men
   - Women to be submissive
   - Women inferior to men
   - Men superior to women
   - Religious rules and restrictions

   (b)
   - Female perspective on spirituality
   - Qualities of care, compassion and forgiveness
   - Understanding of family situations

2. (b) continued
   - Understanding of motherhood
   - Understanding of 'feminine' aspects of God's nature
   - Contribution to female perspective on ethical issues
   - Contribution to female perspective on theological issues

   (c) Explain how gender stereotyping might create problems in society.
   - Discrimination
   - Victimisation
   - Lack of equal opportunities
   - Low self-esteem
   - Denial of human rights
   - Difficult to fulfil potential
   - Injustice in law
   - Injustice in social and political life
   - Loss of democratic freedom

   (d) Religious viewpoints may include:
   - different but equally important
   - religious teaching on roles and equality
   - perceptions of the roles and equality within a religion
   - domestic roles and responsibilities as they relate to equal opportunities
   - the status of women in a religion.

   Other viewpoint may be a differing one from within a religion or a view independent of religion:
   - UN view
   - EOC view
   - EC view
   - national government view.

   Comparison of the two is possible:
   - areas of agreement
   - areas of disagreement
   - identification of common themes
   - strengths of arguments
   - weaknesses of arguments.

3. (a)
   - It is hoped that by the end of the sentence the criminal will have learned to change his/her behaviour.
   - The criminal may be deterred from acting in a similar way in the future.
   - Others may not wish to follow the same course of action.
   - Having learned a lesson, he/she may become a valuable member of society in the future.
   - Reformation brings a complete change of lifestyle.
   - Having deterred such action, members of society may feel safer in their daily lives.
   - Reformation may enable others to learn to forgive.

   (b)
   - Community service orders involve the person compensating society for the wrong behaviour.
   - Community-based tasks make the local environment a better place for all.
   - The person, having repaid society, may be able to make a new beginning.
   - In the process of carrying out the task, the criminal may learn about respect of others and the community.
   - This is an alternative to prison and so is a saving to the community.
   - The person is less likely to associate with hardened criminals during the period of the sentence.

   (c)
   - Some people may feel that it is not right that society should continue to pay to keep the person in prison.
   - If a person has committed a terrible crime, prison is too good for them.

**Religious, Moral and Philosophical Studies
Higher 2006 (New Arrangements) Paper 1 (cont.)**

3. (c) continued

- Life sentence in the UK does not in fact seem to mean a life sentence.
- To lock a person up for life is morally wrong because it offers no hope of reform.
- It is morally wrong to remove all hope from a person.
- The person is still there as a constant reminder to the family of the victim.
- To cage a person for life is to treat the person like an animal.

(d) Retribution could be seen to make others seem as bad as the criminal.

- Retribution does not help in the process of reformation.
- Deterrence is much better than retribution for all.
- Reform of the criminal should be the first moral goal.
- Retribution may not achieve anything worthy so it is of little value.
- Utilitarians might agree that such punishment was good for the happiness of the majority.
- Retribution does not fit well with a code of justice.
- Retribution may impinge on the person's human rights and dignity.
- Some groups might feel that retribution is in the hands of God.
- Some might say that such crimes are so bad that this is the only morally acceptable way for society to act.
- Deterrence and reformation set good examples for others, retribution may not.
- Retribution may in fact be the best deterrent so morally correct in the long-term.
- Modern scientific theory and the study of criminology suggest that reformation should be the first priority.
- Religious people might say that crime is sin and sin should be punished.
- Alternatives can be shown to be more morally acceptable.
- It is not morally acceptable to ignore the needs of the victim.
- Retribution is morally degrading and so cannot be acceptable.

4. (a) • Reproductive
- Designer babies – using germ-line therapy to alter the height, hair or eye colour of a child so that it is more socially acceptable
- Experimental
- Cloning
- Overcoming fertility problems

(b) • Very strict guidelines about the use of embryos.
- Different regulating criteria used for embryos to be used in research and those to be used in treatment.
- Human cloning for reproductive purposes is banned in the UK.
- Unlimited fine and up to a ten-year prison sentence.
- Stem cell research must only be for therapeutic use.
- Governing body set up to monitor all research and the issuing of licences – this is the HFEA (Human Fertilisation and Embryology Authority).
- Permission will only be given to use embryos when the HFEA is satisfied that the project will achieve certain research goals:
  – to increase knowledge about embryo development
  – to increase knowledge about serious disease.
- To enable such knowledge to be applied in developing treatment for serious disease.

(c) • Wrong to play God.
- Should not be allowed to experiment on or with human life to pursue research no matter how groundbreaking – this is a matter of human rights.

4. (c) continued

- Manipulating genes alters our personal and genetic uniqueness.
- People are created to exist in their own right, not as an extension of someone else.
- The genetically engineered child may feel beholding to the sibling they helped to save.
- That it is right to try to help or save the life of another by using this type of therapy.
- That they are not playing God: no designing involved, just selection.
- That it could cure incurable diseases.
- Finding a genetic cure is no different from finding a drug cure.

(d) • Humans do not have the right to play God.
- It is a sin to interfere with the uniqueness of God-given human life.
- All life is sacred including people with disabilities – do they not have a right to be respected and accepted despite their handicap?
- Everyone has limitations and we accept these – it is the combination of these strengths and weaknesses that gives us our individuality.
- We should not control the lives of others; we should accept them as they are and their place in God's plan.
- We should not try to make life on earth perfect, only heaven is perfect.
- Altering genes would alter a person's place in this plan and has no part in religious belief.
- Potentially, this type of therapy could help other people in a similar situation.
- This could be seen from a Utilitarian perspective: by carrying out this research, it could benefit the majority.
- The fact is we can do it and as we have seen already, people are paying for therapeutic and reproductive genetic engineering. It would be better to have clear guidelines and a law controlling it before it becomes subject to abuse.
- We also do not know what the long-term consequences will be.
- If anything went wrong with this type of therapy, it cannot be reversed.
- Liberalists would say that an embryo is not a foetus until fourteen days old.
- However, some religious people believe that life begins at the moment of conception.
- Some religions believe that it is alright to use this technology to cure diseases but not to create humans.
- 70% of the British public support the use of therapeutic and experimental genetic engineering.

5. (a) Any three relevant points, eg:
- easy and more precise in targeting
- can change direction in mid-flight, ie bend
- more predictable, avoiding injury to non-combatants.

(b) Any three relevant points, eg:
- 1997 Ottawa Convention: 84 states signed up to prohibit the use of anti-personnel mines
- 1980: 73 states signed up to the UN convention on Prohibition or Restriction of Use of Certain Conventional Weapons: weapons leaving undetectable fragments in the human body (Protocol I), mines, booby traps and other devices (Protocol II), incendiary weapons (Protocol III), blinding laser weapons (Protocol IV), explosive remnants of war (Protocol V)
- 1925 Geneva Protocol: treaty which prohibited the use of asphyxiating, poisonous or other gases and bacteriological methods of warfare: many states signed but with the reservation that they could retaliate in kind if they or their allies were attacked
- 1856 Hague Conventions (1899 and 1907) (IV) tried to set limits on the conduct of war, especially the use of certain weapons, eg projectiles filled with poisonous gas.

5. (c) Issues, eg:
- is it ever possible to use them without civilian casualties?
- injustice of inevitable shedding of innocent blood
- can weapons ever be proportionate? difficulty of predicting harm and gain
- economic harm caused leads to further suffering
- increasingly difficult to use any kind of weapons without facing the possibility of escalation to broader or even total war
- expenditure preventing constructive development
- right to self-defence
- duty of authorities to protect the welfare of the people entrusted to their care
- we harm others by non-action and encourage the authors of aggression
- is it right to use weapons to attempt to establish peace and justice?

(d) Candidates must relate points to specific teachings of religions, philosophers and organisations, eg:
- basis is fear and threat, therefore morally unacceptable
- cannot lead to true peace
- all energies focused on destructive not constructive development
- this may well aggravate the causes of war and make it more likely
- risk of accidental use with devastating effects
- references to religious scriptures and leaders, philosophers, organisations, reports which have condemned this.

However,
- moral duty to prevent war, especially nuclear, from ever occurring
- duty of citizens to support an effective military strategy
- balance of threat preserves peace
- duty to defend nation/religion
- moral/religious duty to preserve certain beliefs and values, eg justice, freedom
- cannot 'disinvent' them, therefore better to attempt to keep peace through limited possession and control of them
- references which encourage preparing for war or defence

Section 2: Christianity: Belief and Science

1. (a) A description of scientific method, eg:
- method summed up in the following: observation; hypothesis; experiment; verification
- basis of scientific method is empirical evidence
- use of inductive reasoning
- use of deductive reasoning
- three criteria for evaluating theory: agreement; internal relations; comprehensiveness
- scientific method affirms no theory can be proven: coherency, eg alternative theories.

(b)
- Moses on Mount Sinai.
- The supreme revelation of God in Christ.
- Revelation means that God has taken the initiative in revealing something of his attributes to humans.
- Theology would be impossible without a self-revelation of God.
- Revelation is a supernatural act of self-communication – a purposeful act on the part of God.

General and Special Revelation
- General – 'revelatio realis' – a revelation in nature, in human consciousness and in the providential government of the world.
- Special – 'revelatio verbalis' – a revelation embodied in the Bible as the word of God.

1. (b) continued
- General is rooted in creation, addressed to human reason. It finds its purpose in the realisation of the end of his creation – to know God and enjoy communion with Him.
- Special is rooted in the redemptive plan of God – is addressed to man as sinner and can be understood by faith.
- Special revelation gives knowledge of mysteries – Trinity, Incarnation, Redemption. It is not rationally demonstrable but must be accepted by faith.
- The only proper way to obtain perfectly reliable knowledge of God's attributes is by a study of God's self-revelation in Scripture.
- Revelation through the works of God – nature – God as designer and purposer.
- Revelation through the word of God – scripture providing truth in all matters of experience including history and science.

(c)
- Deductive method – things do not always square with experience.
- Faith dependent on personal commitment.
- The method of science based on empirical evidence.
- Belief in the impartiality of science – it begins from a neutral standpoint.
- Scientific method is grounded in fact, experiment and proof.
- Religious questions not testable by observation.
- Dangers of literalism.
- Revelation based on faith but for the religious believer this leads to certainty – certainty born of personal conviction.
- Science can give proof obtained from the best possible evidence – it is a proof, based on our present knowledge, always open to the possibility of future revision.
- Danger of use of models in science and religion.
- Language of religion not disinterested.
- No scientific theory is safe for all time – Ptolemaic view of universe was falsified by Copernicus – the physics of Newton superseded by Einstein.
- Scientific theories ultimately only hypotheses open to refutation.
- Uninterpreted experience leads to misinterpretation.

(d)
- A special application of the Cosmological argument.
- Infers the existence of God from the presence of order.
- Order is seen as a mark of design.
- Coincides with a revival of interest in natural theology.
- Analogy is between the universe and a man-made machine – Paley's watch.
- Human eye cited as evidence/comparison.
- Causal link watch → watchmaker → God.
- Just as design apparent in watch could not have happened by chance, so 'design' in universe – including living creatures/humans – demand a designer to explain them.
- Swinburne: order means world runs according to regular laws. God responsible for scientific laws – the explanation for the orderliness of the universe.

(e)
- key to the theory is 'natural selection'
- within species, individual members may have particular characteristics which help them to survive
- advantages are passed on through reproduction
- over generations the characteristics which improve chances of survival will be found in an increasing number of individuals
- by this process nature selects those most fit to survive.

Religious, Moral and Philosophical Studies
Higher 2006 (New Arrangements) Paper 1 (cont.)

1. (f) • Evolution can be seen as a creative process with God behind it.
   • Evolution shows the power of God and enhances belief.
   • Evolutionary theory explains how life developed, Revelation explains why (complementary)
   • Religious and scientific truth are different and should not be confused (eg Teilhard, Peacocke, Polkinghorne).
   • Anthropic principle supports existence of an intelligent designer.
   • Acceptance by Christians that there is random chance but that the rules were formulated by God.
   • A theistic interventionist approach suggests that evolution is acceptable but God intervenes directly. Body of Adam result of natural selection from other species, but the soul created directly by God.
   • Evolution is the mechanism by which God creates and operates.
   • Vitalism (Bergson) sees the action of God within the evolutionary process.
   • Evolution is purposeful (Peacocke) – God's activity determines the 'final causes' of everything.
   • A problem arises in this debate – how is it possible to relate an autonomous universe with what religious people want to claim as the action of God?

Religious, Moral and Philosophical Studies
Higher 2006 (New Arrangements) Paper 2

Section 1: Buddhism

1. (a) Points may include, eg:
   • The Third Noble Truth – ultimate goal of a Buddhist
   • extinguishing the fires of anger, desire and ignorance
   • unconditioned state of bliss
   • end of craving/ignorance
   • difficult to describe – can only be experienced
   • not a place – not Buddhist heaven.

   (b) This is Samsara. Points may include:
   Lower life:
   • life of suffering/ignorance
   • state of conditioned existence – our actions create conditions for future existence
   • unenlightened actions bring suffering
   • state of ignorance continues while we remain unenlightened
   • all beings linked in web of existence.

   Bondage:
   • we are tied to Samsara by our ignorance
   • tied by three poisons which keep the wheel turning.

   (c) • Father provided luxury so that he would not desire things in order to avoid his asking questions. Hoped he would not ask questions and become a holy man.
   • Became dissatisfied inside palace. Desire to know what was outside. Tempted out of the palace.
   • Lived as a sadhu to try to confront human desires and temptations in order to find Enlightenment.
   • Tempted by Mara (five daughters: pride, greed, ignorance, desire and fear) to give up meditation under Bo tree.
   • Craving was third insight he gained when meditating.
   • Enlightenment is point at which all cravings cease.

   (d) This is Tanha. Points may include:
   • craving is origin of suffering
   • while we are craving, we are not Enlightened
   • we grasp at things we enjoy and want them to be permanent and we suffer when they are not
   • we want to own more of things that make us happy
   • nothing stays the same, so we continue to crave
   • following Dhamma leads to simplicity, to contentment, to decrease in worldly gains and acquisitions
   • Fourth Noble Truth is ending of suffering: only when we stop craving do we achieve inner calm and satisfaction
   • Nibbana is when all cravings cease.

   (e) Reasons why yes:
   • the removal of craving and destruction of attachments and desires are the means to Enlightenment, so it would seem that in any tradition it would be easier to achieve as a monk than as laity because of fewer temptations
   • being a monk allows time to devote to spiritual training necessary for Enlightenment, eg meditation on craving
   • monastic life has fewer distractions so monks can confront greed, hatred and ignorance which lay people have less time to notice or deal with
   • within Theravada, only really possible for monks – stress the need for monastic existence to achieve Enlightenment
   • only monks gain Arahatship.

   Reasons why no:
   • Mahayana believes all beings have the capacity to become enlightened. Desires have to be thrown off for this to happen
   • greater vehicle, so more people benefit from Mahayana practices, so laity can achieve Enlightenment

1. (e) (cont.)
- both monastic and lay Buddhists take refuge in the Three Jewels
- lay Buddhists can still progress spiritually with good effort
- Dhamma embraces every aspect of life – secular too, so laity can work at curbing desires and progressing to Enlightenment
- Enlightenment is only ever achieved by own efforts whether as a monk or as laity.

2.
- Anatta is doctrine of no self.
- It is Anicca applied to people. Nothing in humans is permanent because people are of an impermanent world.
- People are made of a bundle of five skandhas, none of which is permanent.
- Non-acceptance of this leads to suffering.
- It is a wrong understanding of the world to think of self as being at the centre.
- Buddha emphasised need to realise Anatta in order to reach Enlightenment.

SO … belief in Anatta would help because:
- Buddhists would not be trying to satisfy 'self' in seeking Enlightenment: cannot satisfy 'self' because 'self' is not permanent
- self-centredness arises from attachment – this is unenlightened
- negative states of mind result from attachment to self, eg hurt when insulted
- positive states of mind also result from attachment to self, eg happy when praised
- to cultivate Nibbana is not cultivating ego: it is to cultivate a release from the need to satisfy self
- must give up preoccupation with 'me' and 'my needs' to achieve Enlightenment
- must show compassion for others (without doing so for Karmic gain) in order to achieve Enlightenment
- impossible to be selfish and achieve Enlightenment because if cultivated for 'self's' sake it wouldn't be achieved
- living with delusion of a self cannot result in ease of mind
- path to Nibbana involves overcoming obstacles in self.

However:
- other key concepts must also be accepted, eg Anicca.

Section 2: Christianity

1. (a)
- Put on trial and wrongly accused
- Mocked/crown of thorns
- Whipped by the soldiers
- Made to carry his cross to the place of execution
- Nailed to the cross
- His dying
- Suffering of knowing his innocence

(b)
- They gather together on Sunday to worship and give thanks.
- They follow his teachings.
- They try to live their lives by his example.
- They celebrate Mass/Communion. (Full answer on main elements of either can gain full marks.)
- They love their neighbours as themselves.
- They live in a sense of forgiveness and hope for the future.
- They believe that Jesus' death has defeated death, so they have hope of eternal life.
- Easter Sunday is the most important event in the Christian calendar.
- Common symbol of the crucifix/cross.

(c)
- By repentance of past sins and errors, they can begin again.
- Acceptance of Jesus as a personal Lord and Saviour brings them support.
- By submission to his will gives this present life meaning and purpose.

1. (c) (cont.)
- By living in a state of constant communion with him/prayer and action, they feel his constant support and help in times of need.
- A relationship with Jesus gives meaning to other relationships.
- It restores the broken relationship between humans and God.
- It also restores the broken relationship between other humans.
- It leads to concern for others in acts of charity.
- Candidates may develop the consequences of the Fall.
- Alienation restored in Christ.
- Promise of eternal life/end of death.

(d)
- Life after death with God
- Life in all its fullness for eternity
- A new view of this present world
- A restored relationship with God
- Belief in eternal life
- Atonement/oneness with God
- Spiritual life now and after death in the holy spirit
- Descriptions of Heaven/Hell

(e)
- New Testament testimony to this fact
- Belief that resurrection is the first fruits for believers
- Belief that it was Jesus' death and resurrection that restores a relationship with God
- It is by following Jesus that wholeness is restored
- Leading a moral life depends on the help of Jesus
- Jesus alone heals morally, physically and spiritually
- Freedom from sin comes through Jesus
- Life in Jesus is life in a new spirit
- Jesus alone can rescue people from the human condition
- Christ is with them moment by moment
- The healing ministry of Jesus.

2.
- Important because Jesus taught about the importance of Judgement.
- It helps Christians to understand the compassion of God.
- God is all-powerful/omnipotent.
- Only God has the right to final judgement.
- Sheep will be separated from the goats.
- A proper and fair judgement for those who have lived by the teaching of Jesus.
- Important in that it could be an impetus for evangelism.
- It is an incentive to live the good life.
- Gives direction and purpose to the here and now.
- Without this Christianity has little to offer humanity.
- Reinforces beliefs in life and death.

But it may not help because:
- Unimportant because the Christian life is not based on the fear of death
- Christian life is a response to Christ
- Service is given in gratitude for what Jesus has done
- Different groups have different emphasis on this topic.

**Religious, Moral and Philosophical Studies
Higher 2006 (New Arrangements) Paper 2 (cont.)**

Section 3: Hinduism

1. (a) •   Brahman is in everything
   •   Universe is Brahman
   •   We all have Brahman within
   •   The atman is Brahman and vice versa.

   (b) •   Beyond our definitions
   •   Nothing can affect Brahman
   •   Brahman cannot be destroyed
   •   Above and beyond the universe
   •   Other than the universe
   •   Remote.

   (c) Knowledge and Understanding:
   •   Path of devotion
   •   Practice of puja
   •   Worship of personal deity
   •   Redirection emotion of love to God.

   Analysis and Evaluation:
   •   Transfers culturally
   •   Most practical for 21st century
   •   Easy to understand
   •   No restrictions on caste
   •   Harnesses natural emotions
   •   Does not involve self-mortification
   •   Can be part of everyday life
   •   Kirshna recommended as the best.

   (d) •   Vedas contain the truth
   •   Vedas explain the nature of the universe
   •   Vedas contain advice for living
   •   Vedas are the holiest of all scripture
   •   Vedas are revealed by Brahman.

   (e) Knowledge and Understanding:
   •   Role of guru in worship
   •   Role of guru in festivals
   •   Role of guru in rites of passage
   •   Role of guru in spiritual teaching.

   Analysis and Evaluation:
   •   Initiates the spiritual search
   •   Transmits his spiritual power
   •   Transmits spiritual truth
   •   Guides along the path of Enlightenment
   •   Sets an example of how to do it
   •   Dispels spiritual darkness
   •   Leads the individual to the truth
   •   Much depends on the path followed, for some the guru is not important.

2. 4 marks for a description of karma:
   •   good acts
   •   bad acts
   •   pitiless law of existence
   •   affects samsara
   •   varna and ashrama.

   Discussion of karma as related to:
   •   importance in the margas, eg good karma is to follow one's path
   •   importance in dharma, eg good karma is to follow one's duty
   •   importance in the human condition, eg we all have to act
   •   importance in the goals, eg renunciation
   •   importance in the means, eg caste.

   There would be disagreement with this view:
   •   Avidya is more important
   •   got to understand how the karma fits into our ignorance
   •   Avidya destroys desire associated with karma
   •   transience could hold the key to Hinduism
   •   accept all is transient, even karma, to understand universe

2. continued
   •   understanding of the self (atman) is the key, eg separate self from ego and karma's effect falls away
   •   Moksha, the goal of life, transcends karma

Section 4: Islam

1. (a) •   That they should be ready to speak with Allah in prayer and should be clean to be in his presence
   •   This infers the ritual cleansing of Wuzu
   •   There are many rules about this ritual
   •   That it is associated with certain other actions
   •   Association with certain acts and people put a Muslim in a state of uncleanliness
   •   Points to the future with Allah, is a state of purification.

   (b) •   Brings the Muslim closer to Allah
   •   Combines the body and soul
   •   Brings the individual a sense of peace and tranquillity
   •   For the community a sense of brotherhood and fellowship
   •   Personal discipline
   •   Changes a person's life and their perspective of themselves and others
   •   Promotes patience, courage, hope and confidence
   •   Prepares the Muslim for the trials of this life and the future with Allah.

   (c) •   Submission is the very heart of Islam
   •   Meaning of the word Islam
   •   To submit to Allah is a test of faith
   •   Also a test of character
   •   Wrongdoing leads to suffering so obedience is important to follow the correct path
   •   Through obedience people learn to accept Allah as compassionate
   •   Helps in conformation to the laws
   •   It is only through such obedience to the will of Allah that they will inherit eternal life
   •   They will learn to be better people by submitting to the will of Allah
   •   Life will be happier for all with such submission and obedience
   •   Less suffering will result
   •   Allah in return will offer his support
   •   Paradise is guaranteed to those who submit to the will of Allah
   •   They will be following the good example of Muhammad
   •   Ishan and taqwa as the beginning of true submission
   •   Covers all aspects of life
   •   The Qu'ran states on many occasions that all must submit to the will of Allah.

   (d) •   Faith without action is meaningless
   •   All life is to be praise to Allah
   •   All will one day be answerable to Allah for all actions
   •   Day of Judgement
   •   Nobody, not even Muhammad, knows when this day will be
   •   Record of deeds kept by the angels
   •   These will be handed over at the last day
   •   Faithful are purified – evildoers will suffer
   •   This is an encouragement to live the good life
   •   Encourages the practice of the Five Pillars
   •   Gives meaning and purpose to life
   •   It holds the promise of eternal life.

   (e) •   Everything in the universe is under the control of Allah
   •   Allah has granted humans the right to choose their own actions
   •   Freewill is this right to choose
   •   It is what makes us human
   •   Our days are all counted/predestined

1. (*e*) continued

- Everything is known to Allah
- Human beings are not governed in the same way as the natural law of the world
- Misuse of freewill deprives people of right of entry to paradise
- Misuse results in suffering
- Causes alienation from Allah if used wrongly
- Causes alienation between people likewise
- Misuse results in conflict
- People who walk in the dark will be blind to the truth
- If we do not wish to be burned, we must stay out of the fire
- Misuse of freewill affects people physically as well as morally
- It brings penalty on the day of judgement.

2. Any two of the following:

Kalimah and Shahadah
- Importance of the recitation of the Shahadah
- This is the way of worship

Zakah
- The giving of charity at least once per year

Sawm
- Fasting during the month of Ramadan

Hajj
- The annual pilgrimage to Mecca.

The benefits to the individual and community of the chosen two.

Kalimah and Shahadah
- Strong sense of community inspired by this
- The basis of Islam is submission for the whole community and the individual
- Way into worship for the community and the individual
- Therefore a benefit
- But it could become mere repetition and so of little benefit
- May take away individual actions.

Zakah
- Cleanses the individual of love of money
- Purifies the individual
- Encourages compassion for all
- Can be seen as all that is required, therefore can be restrictive of action
- Could encourage false sense of pride in the individual and the community
- Equality for all
- Money helps not only individuals but all of the community
- A once a year thing so forgotten for the rest of the year
- May engender an inward-looking community.

Sawm
- Develops individual self-control
- Overcomes selfishness for all of the community
- Builds up spiritual self/individual and community
- Shared ordeal
- Self-righteousness can easily be fostered
- Develops the moral life
- Sense of individual willpower
- Could become inward-looking.

Hajj
- Develops a strong sense of faith
- Forgiveness of Allah to the individual and all the community
- Sense of self to become a pilgrim now and in all life
- More aware of the soul and the fragility of life
- Can engender a feeling of the only one true religion
- Having accomplished it may mean no further need for action.

Section 5: Judaism

1. (*a*)
- Messiah will be a man – prophet, teacher, leader
- Descendent of David
- Peace will reign
- Lead Jewish people back to the land of Israel
- Either because world is good enough – or too evil.

(*b*)
- Ritual observance, eg Shabbat, Kashrut
- Festivals – Pesach, Sukkot
- Mezuzah, tefillin
- Brit Milah
- Lashon Harah
- Study of Torah and Talmund.

(*c*)
- Both given to Moses on Mount Sinai
- Written Law unchanged
- Oral Law is explanations and interpretations
- Oral Law grows and develops.

(*d*)
- Biblical teachings set out to ensure justice and fairness to all
- Prophets fought for social righteousness
- Justice applies to all spheres of life, eg business
- Basic belief is that God deals justly with his creation
- Special consideration for the weak and defenceless.

(*e*)
- World to come – where souls go after death
- Ultimate reward for righteous Jews
- Enjoy God's presence, absence of anything negative
- Observance of mitzvoth in this life influences world to come
- Working towards peace in this world
- Opportunity for sincere repentance
- Tenakh makes little mention of world to come.

2. Creation/image of God, eg:
- everything in Creation is as God willed it
- man given sovereignty over nature
- God's nature: omniscient, omnipotent, omnipresent
- creator, father, king, judge, teacher
- human beings reflect God's nature
- man has moral capacity, reason, free will
- man can love God and have a spiritual bond.

The implications of this belief for Jews, eg:
- creation is ongoing and moving towards fulfilment of a purpose
- responsibility to follow God's guidelines for life
- to resist the yetzer harah
- strengthen spiritual bond through prayer, teshuvah
- gain closeness to God through ritual observance
- show love for God through love for others, Golden Rule
- await the coming of the Messiah/Messianic Age.

Section 6: Sikhism

1. (*a*) Three relevant points, eg:
- God as the creator of all that exists
- God as the controlling power behind all events and circumstances in a person's life
- God's Grace is needed for spiritual development, a person cannot make progress without it
- everyone has free will and must exercise their choices in the circumstances God has given them.

(*b*) Two uses, eg:
- Guru referring to all, or one of, the ten Sikh Gurus who first taught/communicated the Sikh faith.
- Guru referring to God as the True Guru, source of all wisdom.

Religious, Moral and Philosophical Studies
Higher 2006 (New Arrangements) Paper 2 (cont.)

1. (c) Any relevant description of **one** way in which a Sikh person worships God, eg:
   - community worship – takes place in a Gurdwara throughout the day (in some areas at set times); washing before visiting Gurdwara, removing shoes, head covered; bowing before the Guru Granth Sahib and giving an offering; sitting with others on the floor and listening to Granthi reading from Guru Granth Sahib; sharing karah prashad and langar in recognition of God within all/all equal.
   - private devotion – following a daily routine of prayer and meditation; rising early (the 'ambrosial hour'), washing and meditating on God's name/Naam until sunrise; mentally or verbally repeating God's name/Naam while carrying out daily work/duties; prayers and meditation at the end of the day; reading and studying passages from the Guru Granth Sahib; Khalsa Sikhs have additional devotional duties (five set times).
   - may also refer to sewa (service) as form of worship or caring for Guru Granth Sahib.

   (d) Knowledge and Understanding of transmigration, eg:
   - all human beings have a soul/atma which is part of God
   - the soul journeys through many lives and forms before becoming human and having the opportunity to reunite with God.

   Further explanation of transmigration, eg:
   - birth as a human is unique because only in human form can the soul reunite with God
   - the soul's progress is determined by the law of karma which is part of the created order
   - good karma brings the soul closer to reunion, bad karma takes the soul further away from God
   - karma is created through a person's thoughts and actions
   - consciously acting in harmony with God's Will cancels out all previous karma and avoids new karma being created. This leaves the human open to reunion with God.

   (e) Definition of Sewa as 'service in a spirit of emotional detachment/without thought of reward' (or equivalent).

   Any relevant explanation of the importance of Sewa, eg
   - Sewa is of equal importance with simran (devotion/worship) in helping Sikhs to progress towards reunion with God – one without the other is pointless
   - involves service within the Sikh community (Gurdwara or wider Sikh community) and also to all humanity in recognition of the belief that God is within all creation
   - by serving creation/others, Sikhs believe that they are also serving God who is within all creation.

   (f) Description of the final goal as 'merging/reunion with God'. Any other relevant facts to expand on this, eg:
   - involves reunion of the soul/atma with its original source
   - phrase 'peace and tranquillity'
   - can only ultimately be achieved by the grace of God
   - phrase 'my Lord and Master has become merciful'
   - cannot be fully described, can only be experienced.

   Further relevant explanation, eg:
   - based on the belief that, at the creation of the universe, God infused Self into all creation and is the soul or divine spark within all creation
   - human beings can help themselves through meditation (simran) and service (sewa)
   - phrase 'sing the Praises of his Lord'
   - reunion with God not after death – Jivan Mukti
   - state of peace/contentment ('I have found peace and tranquillity')

1. (f) continued
   - all material and worldly concerns are irrelevant ('my struggle has ended')
   - a state of equipoise where pain and pleasure are experienced with equal detachment (sahej).

2. A description of Sikh beliefs regarding the importance of fulfilling the duties of a householder, eg:
   - all creation is part of God and only by serving/engaging with creation can a person reunite with God
   - Sikh Gurus taught that it is only by engaging with the world (which is part of God) that one can truly serve God
   - family/community life is an important way of engaging with the world
   - Sikhs reject the route of withdrawal/asceticism (may include an example/anecdote).

   In agreement with statement, eg:
   - many temptations and distractions are involved in living as a householder (wealth, becoming emotionally attached, contemporary pressure to 'succeed' (five evils))
   - it is very difficult not to become emotionally attached to members of your family (eg children/parents)
   - daily practical duties involved in family life can cause frustration or distraction from the spiritual goals of life
   - the idea of engaging with the world in a spirit of detachment may go against modern emphasis on self-realisation/gratification.

   In disagreement with statement:
   - by engaging with the world a Sikh is constantly reminded of 'God within all creation' (reinforces belief)
   - gives a sense of appreciation of the struggles/experiences of others and can promote compassion
   - avoids the danger of becoming divorced from reality
   - fits with modern ideas of the importance of commitment to/engagement with others.
   - Candidates may include examples of the work of individual Sikhs/Sikh communities in improving/serving the world around them.

2007 Religious, Moral and Philosophical Studies
Higher Paper 1

SECTION 1

1. (a) A maximum of 2 marks for an account of the dilemma.
    A maximum of 2 marks for formula.
    Other points may include eg:
    • concerns the origin of morality
    • a description of the context
    • centres around the issue of what it is that makes an
      action right or good
    • are actions good in themselves or are they good because
      an external authority (eg God) commands them?
    • Socrates implies that actions are good in themselves
    • Formula – 'Is what is good loved by the Gods…'.

(b) KU may include eg:
    • treat others in the same way that you would want them
      to treat you
    • examples from specific religions or philosophical
      traditions may be referred to
    • it may be noted that it is found in all religious traditions
      and cited by humanist or other non-religious thinkers.

(c) A description of the ideas of Bentham, Mill, Singer eg:
    • Utilitarian ethics focus on consequences of actions
      rather than actions themselves
    • good actions promote the greatest happiness/pleasure of
      the greatest number
    • based on the assumption/idea that happiness/pleasure is
      the desired end of all human activity
    • Act/Rule distinction
    • Teleological as apposed to deontological.

2. (a) • Financially dependent on men.
    • Equal opportunities in education/training.
    • Limited promotion prospects.
    • Career or family – not both.
    • Barred from 'men's jobs'.

(b) • Less pressure to be 'breadwinner'.
    • More freedom for leisure/time with family.
    • Increased family income.
    • Breaks down barriers between the sexes.
    • Opportunities for men to share in traditionally female
      roles.

(c) • Vision for fairer society.
    • Campaigns on range of gender equality issues.
    • Raises public awareness of issues.
    • But only deals with sex discrimination.
    • Needs better funding.
    • Could be more independent of government.
    • Pay gap and glass ceiling still exist.
    • Could be more vocal in political debate.

(d) (i) Candidates must refer to specific religious teaching
      and/a viewpoint(s) dealing with the issue of economic
      equality/inequality between men and women. Points
      must relate to the different viewpoints found in either
      one or two religions. A maximum of 4 marks may be
      awarded for straightforward description of teachings
      and/a viewpoint(s).

2. (d) (ii) • different interpretations of scripture
      • teachings of different founders/leaders
      • influence of leading devotees and/or organisations
        within the religion
      • different traditions expressing a variety of views
      • weightings given to scripture, tradition, contemporary
        views
      • place of individual conscience in decision-making
      • historic/cultural development of a religion.

3. (a) • Stayed in the same building as Christie the mass
        murderer.
    • Not very clever and he was prone to telling lies.
    • Police found the bodies of his wife and child in the
      building.
    • Confessed to the murders after lengthy questioning.
    • Evidence unreliable.
    • Police omitted evidence that might have helped him.
    • Tried and sentenced to death.
    • He was executed.
    • Christie later confessed to the murder of Beryl Evans
      and many others.
    • Christie was executed.
    • Later Evans was pardoned.

(b) • It states that Capital Punishment removes human
        dignity.
    • Nobody has the right to take away another person's life,
      not even governments.
    • Capital Punishment and all the appeals is a form of
      mental torture and so wrong.
    • All human beings are born equal and should be treated
      with respect.
    • The very act of execution is degrading.
    • Could be said to be unhelpful because seems one sided.
    • Gives very clear guidance.

(c) Maximum of 2 marks for describing methods of execution.
    • No method of execution can be shown beyond doubt
      not to cause pain.
    • States who carry out execution are performing legal
      murder – this is immoral.
    • Some non-religious people may quote the Golden
      Rule.
    • Non-religious people might agree that to kill is wrong.
    • Where people are permitted to view the execution is
      even more immoral.
    • Removal of human dignity is immoral.
    • Leaving no room for new evidence of innocence.
    • Some might argue it is not what they deserve.
    • Some might argue it is too lenient and so not morally
      acceptable.
    • Once execution has been carried out the state may be
      reluctant to accept they have killed an innocent person.

(d) (i) Examples might include:
      • Buddhists believe that all killing is wrong because it
        opposes parts of the 8-fold path. Specific examples
        could be cited.
      • Judaism might argue that it was correct because the
        OT states that there should be an eye for an eye.
      • Examples from OT where God tells them to execute
        enemies.
      • Christians might take a similar stance and groups
        within might take opposing stances.

2007 Religious, Moral and Philosophical Studies Higher Paper 1 (cont.)

3. (d) (ii) Examples might include:
- The Buddhist argument might be a strength in that it might result in less suffering.
- It might be a weakness in the face of terrorism or dictators
- Ghandi argued that an eye for an eye results in the whole world being blind
- Candidates might argue for or against the idea of Shariah Law. That it is barbaric or that it might serve as a deterrent
- The concept of forgiveness might be argued as a strength or a weakness related to certain stances and viewpoints
- The concept of reformation is important and a strength in many religions
- Is such a concept present in capital punishment?
- Some religions argue that judgement belongs to God

4. (a) Voluntary
- Patient requests action to end his/her life.
- Request that life-saving treatment be withdrawn.
- Patient is in full knowledge that this will lead to death.

Involuntary
- Life ended without the patient's consent.
- Patient is too sick, weak or unconscious to make decision for themselves.

(b) Explain how the UK Law on euthanasia could apply in John's case.
- For all euthanasia to be justified it must be part of medical practice.
- It is still officially illegal in the UK although there is no direct law dealing with euthanasia.
- UK Law does not allow us to kill a human to end their suffering.
- Patient's consent does not provide a defence for the doctor in the UK.
- Anyone assisting deliberate euthanasia would be liable for murder, which may be reduced to manslaughter on the basis of diminished responsibility.
- Seen as an extension of the Suicide Act of 1961 which permits personal autonomy to choose to take your own life.
- Forbids the involvement of a third party.
- Although illegal to take another's life, some doctors may practice a form of 'passive' euthanasia to ease a person's suffering.

(c) How helpful would the BMA guidelines on euthanasia be in this case?
- BMA does not support voluntary euthanasia.
- BMA guidelines are there to protect and help the doctors.
- They allow a consistency in decision making where there has been a grey area before.
- They help to standardise the situation so that every doctor is working within the same framework.
- Guidelines help to reassure patients and family that these difficult decisions are made thoughtfully and sensitively.
- Maintain close discussion with relatives.
- BMA sees a difference in actively terminating a life and treating a patient in a manner that in the end will result in death.
- Supports the doctor in their duty to ensure that a patient dies with dignity and with as little suffering as possible.
- Hippocratic oath to preserve life and to develop the correct doctor-patient relationship, which is to guide and inform the patient's choices.
- Have to be very careful as any decision made about euthanasia cannot be reversed.

4. (d) (i)
- Sanctity is defined in the dictionary as 'Sacred or inviolability'
- Human life is sacred and cannot be treated lightly
- Anything that threatens a human life is questioning the sanctity of life
- Sanctity of life issues include Abortion and Euthanasia which are about the ending of life
- Many religious people believe that only God has the right to take away life

(ii)
- Sanctity of life.
- Issue of personhood.
- The image of God.
- Only God can take life away.
- Life is a gift from God.
- Murder.
- Quality of life.
- Personal autonomy.
- The rights of a person, individual freedom of choice.
- When is life not worth living?
- How much suffering should a person be allowed to endure?
- It allows a person to make a choice to die with dignity.
- If euthanasia is legalised would this not lead to a slippery slope or wedge argument.
- There will always be those who exploit a weaker rule.
- What begins with good intentions may end in an undesirable result.
- Autonomy has limits – no one can be allowed to undermine the rights of another.
- Recognising the right to die would have a knock-on effect for the rest of society.
- Societies attitude to death would change, as would its attitude to old age, illness and disability.
- It would undermine the patient's trust in doctors.

5. (a)
- Dismissed from his job.
- Arrested, tried and jailed.
- Beaten up in the street.
- Ostracised by the community.

(b)
- Process involving dialogue/bargaining with a view to finding terms of agreement to resolve conflict.
- Gives peace a chance.
- One way to explore all peaceful means before considering violent conflict as a last resort.
- Sometimes only means available to weakest.

(c)
- Conscience tells him it is wrong to take innocent lives.
- War is unjust – it causes innocent suffering.
- No situation can be improved by violence.
- Violence only breeds more violence.
- The damaging effects of war are too high a price to pay for victory.

(d) Candidates may refer to a number of articles in the Charter including 39, 41, 42, 51, 53. They may also illustrate points by reference to specific historical examples.
- Origin of UN/Purpose of UN
- Provides an agreed framework for international law on war.
- Has the support of powerful member states and their forces.
- Allows economic and diplomatic sanctions to be employed to enforce its decisions
- Has power to use UN forces to restore international peace and security, if sanctions prove ineffective.
- Recommendations may be ignored.
- Sanctions may aggravate problem for ordinary civilians.
- Time consuming and bureaucratic.

5. (e) (i)
- Two main frameworks within Christianity ie Just War theory, consistent pacifism
- Three conditions of Just War theory laid down by St Thomas Aquinas in 13th century ie War must only be started and controlled by state/ruler; must be a just cause; those attacked deserve it; war must be fought to promote good or avoid evil. Peace and justice must be restored afterwards
- Two conditions added later ie war must be last resort; all other possible ways of solving problem must be tried; must be proportionality in the way the war is fought
- Christian pacifists eg the Quakers would argue we have a higher duty to God to protect and preserve human life
- Seed of Christ in the heart of every individual
- All children of God
- Violence is incompatible with Jesus' teaching
- Sermon on Mount teaches to love enemies and forgive persecutors; 'turn the other cheek; meet evil with good'
- Conditions that support Jihad in Islam ie only called for by a religious leader; in defence of Islam; in order to overthrow oppressive rulers; to preserve ability to live and worship freely
- Jihad is about defence not aggression
- Buddhism places great emphasis on non-violence at every level
- The Buddha taught it is necessary to act non-violently and non-co-operatively in the face of violence
- Evil to be actively opposed by non-violent means

(ii) Arguments based on effective defence:
- war being just
- historical/cultural development of a religion
- God endorsing war
- scriptural justification of war
- relevant teachings of founder, leaders, reports, recommendations etc
- responsibility for community, nation, religion.

Arguments based on ineffective defence:
- traditions of pacifism within religion
- scriptural justification for non-violence
- sanctity or value of life
- inconsistent with teachings on care of environment
- inappropriate in a nuclear age.

SECTION 2

(a)
- Big Bang theory.
- Theories of evolution/Darwin's discoveries.
- Discoveries in astronomy.
- Discoveries in cosmology.
- Discoveries in biology.
- Archaeological evidence/Palaeontological Evidence.

(b)
- Humans are at the centre of creation.
- Universe created for human beings.
- God reveals himself to human beings.
- God has a special role for human beings.
- God loves human beings more than anything else.
- God has given human beings a special purpose.
- God has allowed human beings to have a relationship with him.
- God has imbued human beings with soul.

(c) Scientific method
- depends on observation, hypothesis, prediction and verification.
- Observes the concrete.
- Open to change.
- Open to verification.
- Truths revealed are true until something better comes along.
- Objective.

(c) (cont.)
Revelation
- Interpretation of events is important.
- Truths are eternal.
- Does not submit to usual rules of verification.
- Faith required.
- Subjective.

(d)
- Outline of Paley's argument for full marks.
- The conclusion that the watch had been designed and made would not be weakened if one had never seen a watch before.
- The existence of a designer and maker of the watch would not be negated if the watch went wrong on occasions or did not work at all.
- The fact that the watch had been designed and made would not be negated if there were parts of the watch whose workings were not understood.
- Something as complex as a watch could not appear out of nowhere.
- Same applies to the universe and life forms.

(e)
- God revealed his word to humans.
- God's word is infallible.
- Why would God not speak the truth in the Bible?
- God's word is plain and simple.
- Science contradicts Biblical understanding of creation.
- If you question one part of the Bible you have to question it all.
- The Bible is timeless; truths apply to all ages.
- The evidence for the Big Bang and evolution is by no means conclusive.

(f)
- Views of scientists who are Christians eg Peacocke; Polkinghorne – theistic evolution.
- Bible has to be seen in its cultural context.
- Bible is a record of spiritual experience.
- Bible is not a science book.
- Bible authors did not write it as science.
- Interpretation could be inconsistent – which bits should be literal and which should be symbolic.
- Ancient people taught through myths and stories, Bible does that.
- Literal interpretation can quickly discredit the Bible.
- Outline of non-literal interpretation plus analysis.

(g) Credit can be given for a description of either or both the Big Bang theory and evolutionary theories for KU. The Big Bang providing it is in the context of evolution.
KU
- Revelation.
- Big Bang theory
- Theories of evolution – This will be acceptable even though candidates will have covered this in part (a).
AE
Points against the statement
- Revelation is at odds with evolution.
- Revelation does not account for much scientific data.
- Science deals in facts not emotions and beliefs.
- Revelation always wants to bring God into the debate.
- What other explanation is there? Life is here ... end of story.
- Science does not make absolute statements – it has the humility to be tentative in its assertions.
- Science has nothing to say about revelation and vice versa.
- Creation scientists would be uncomfortable with statement.
- Creation scientists would go for Noahaic Flood explanation of evolutionary evidence.

2007 Religious, Moral and Philosophical Studies
Higher Paper 1 (cont.)

(g) (cont.)

Points for the statement

- More to human origins than scientific facts.
- Evolutionary theory is full of belief too.
- Revelation can explain the purpose behind our existence, science cannot do this.
- Revelation looks for purpose not causes – universe is full of cause and purpose.
- World can be interpreted in more than just a factual way.
- Literalists should be discounted, most Christians do not see revelation in this way and can therefore accept aspects of evolution.
- Evidence of design in evolution.
- Anthropic principle could be discussed.
- Religion and science ask complimentary questions.
- Many Christians accept discoveries of science.
- Christians use science to attach purpose to causes.
- Science uses religion to attach causes to purpose.
- The statement is extreme, there is plenty of agreement in between extremes.

2007 Religious, Moral and Philosophical Studies
Higher Paper 2

Section 1: Buddhism

1. (a)
- Impermanence – nothing lasts forever.
- Universal law covering all universe including dhamma.
- Everything constantly changing and becoming something else.
- One of three Marks of Existence along with anatta and dukkha.
- Some things change slowly, some things fast.
- All things inter-related by anicca as all are constantly changing and this creates a constantly changing relationship of one thing to another ... inter-dependent.

(b) Briefly describe the other two Marks of Existence.

Anatta
- Doctrine of 'no-self'.
- Anicca as applied to people.
- Nothing about a person stays the same.
- Can't have a soul or atman.
- Made up of five skhandas.

Dukkha
- Unsatisfactoriness.
- Contact with the unpleasant brings suffering.
- Separation from the pleasant brings suffering.
- Physical/mental/emotional pain.

(c) What do Buddhists understand by samsara?
- Cycle of rebirth.
- Goal of Buddhists is to gain better samsaric rebirth to reach nibbana.
- Proximal goal for lay Buddhists in theravadin tradition.
- Some mahayanan schools see nibbana and samsara as indistinguishable.
- State of dependent origination.
- While in samsara, we are in a state of constant suffering – dukkha.
- Conditioned by karma in previous lifetimes.
- Trapped in continuous cycle until escape by reaching Enlightenment.

(d)
- Not accepting anicca leads to illusion of permanence which causes craving and attachment.
- Accepting anicca leads to lessening of suffering.
- Not accepting anicca links to bad karma in the form of hatred, greed etc (three poisons).
- Three poisons are centre of wheel of samsara, turning the wheel.
- Delusion and non-acceptance of impermanence lead to suffering caused by attachment.
- Being attached shows ignorance of Buddhist way and keeps people tied to cycle of rebirth.
- Rebirth will continue until one learns not to be attached.

(e) *KU content*
- The true treasure would be found in gaining self harmony by following the Buddhist way.
- Living a Buddhist life following the Dhamma – the teachings.
- Following the example of the Buddha – the one who founded the teachings.
- Right Path – the method that will lead to nibbana.
- Enlightenment is the ultimate treasure.

EA content
- 3 Jewels are all seen as refuges to help Buddhist achieve nibbana, so all are valuable in themselves. All are necessary.
- These will help eliminate suffering, so have true value.
- True treasures are not things that have 'value' in material sense – the real treasure is the Buddhist way.
- Ultimate 'treasure' is nibbana itself – nothing greater.

1. (*f*) • There is a continuity from life to life but no idea of separate 'self' identities, because there is no 'self'.
- There is a causal connection between samsaric lifetimes.
- Karmic influence or energy links from life to life.
- If we don't accept anatta, we will remain self-illusioned, so our actions will be selfish, leading to rebirth.
- Eg a candle flame lights the next candle and causes it to burn, but does not become the new flame.

2. • To outsiders, stream enterers – set on addressing own human condition to progress to nibbana and escape samsaric suffering.
- Behave in a moral way to keep karma good to suit 'self's' progression towards nibbana.
- Theravadins might be accused by Mahayanans of selfishness because aim is to achieve nibbana – arahat.
- Buddha paved way for arahat – no ultimate compassion for others until boddhisatva ideal.
- Possible selfishness of only monks achieving Enlightenment.
- Also selfishness of expecting laity to support monks in 'easy' lifestyle.
- However, can't be selfish because of belief in the no self.
- Wouldn't achieve Enlightenment if they were selfish.
- Buddha's aim was to help all sentient beings.
- Laity gain karma from supporting monks.
- Road to arahathood is moral therefore helps all other beings.
- Monks teach others to help them on road to nibbana.
- Won't achieve Enlightenment if being moral only to benefit 'self'.
- Mahayanans – not selfish (compassion for others led to boddhisatva ideal).
- All can gain Enlightenment in mahayanan Buddhism.

Section 2: Christianity

1. (*a*) • Outline of story and/or consequences
- Banishment from the garden led to a life of toil.
- Alienation from creation.
- Alienation from each other.
- Suffering and death.
- Relationship between humans and God broken.
- Constant state of temptation enters the human condition.

(*b*) • Some may think it means being born again.
- For others new life in Jesus.
- The ability to speak in tongues.
- A close daily relationship with Jesus.
- Jesus as personal saviour.
- Forgiveness of all past sins.
- The ability to heal and help others.
- A turning away from evil acts.
- The ability to preach.
- Help in times of trouble and need.

(*c*) • So that they may live in fellowship with him.
- That they may inherit eternal life.
- That they may be free from future punishment.
- That they may be with him in heaven.
- That life will be better for them now.
- The Kingdom of God may become a reality.
- Jesus taught that they should do this.
- The Bible says this time and again.

1. (*d*) • Stopping doing wrong.
- Following the teachings of Jesus.
- Living by the Ten Commandments.
- Following the Golden Rule.
- Giving their lives over to Jesus.
- Being 'born again'.
- Being baptised into the fellowship of the Church.
- Admitting past sins.
- Repentance.
- Belief in the word of God.
- Belief in action.
- Helping others.
- Acceptance of salvation.
- Believing Jesus died for forgiveness for all.

(*e*) • Worship helps to build the community of Christians.
- Eucharist builds up fellowship one with another.
- The worshippers learn about the life and teachings of Jesus.
- The mission of the Church will be strengthened through the preaching of the word.
- Aware of judgement and heaven and hell.
- Prayer will be a constant help.
- Sense of community will be engendered.
- What is meant by worship?
- What do we mean by Kingdom of God?

2. • Jesus taught about judgement.
- Sheep and goats.
- Good life will be rewarded.
- Bad life will be condemned.
- Emphasis on the threat of hell for some.
- Incentive to good life.
- Justice for all.
- Give purpose to life.
- Spur for evangelism.
- Without this Christianity offers society nothing.
- Motivation to follow Jesus teaching.
- Hope of life after death.
- Therefore hope for the future.
- Gods' justice seen to be fair.
- Contrast with the world.

Could also be stated
- Christian life not dependent on reward.
- Response to Jesus' love.
- Gratitude for salvation.
- Might lead to neglect of the here and now.
- Removal of hope.
- Other things more important.
- The moral life.
- God's love.
- Belief in incarnation.

Section 3: Hinduism

1. (*a*) • Cannot be described.
- It is an experience.
- Brings complete bliss.
- Requires concentration.
- Requires meditation.
- Requires practice.
- Mind becomes one with Brahman.
- Requires detachment.
- Requires renunciation.

2007 Religious, Moral and Philosophical Studies
Higher Paper 2 (cont.)

1. *(b)*
- Concentration.
- Renunciation.
- Self-discipline.
- Encourages people to live a moral life.
- Helps to detach people from everyday life.

(c)
- Life is full of misery and suffering.
- Universe is transient, impermanent.
- Painful to be stuck in the cycle of rebirth.
- Bliss is gained on escape from samara.
- Existence is maya, what's the point of living in an illusion?
- Anything is better than the present existence.
- All will make sense of liberation from samsara.
- End of dharma.

(d) KU
- Moksha is the release from cycle of samsara.
- Recognition of ones of brahman and atman.
- Renunciation of the jiva.
- State of bliss.
- Can be achieved at death in some traditions.
- Can be achieved during life in other traditions.

AE
- Highly abstract.
- Can be very intellectual.
- Philosophical ideal not a practical reality.
- Beyond most people.
- More materialistic world.
- Attachment to the phenomenal world.
- Unwillingness to renounce jiva.
- Possible traditional caste restrictions.

(e) KU
- Four types of dharma - universal, human, social and individual.
- Found in the vedas.
- Morality is an important part of it.
- Caste is associated with dharma.
- Ashrama is associated with dharma.

AE
- Everyone has a role.
- Duties take precedence over rights.
- Linked to karma.
- Linked to samsara.
- Contributes to a balanced society.
- Recognises different stages and approaches to quest for liberation.
- Vedas and Gita emphasise dharma.
- Moral behaviour promotes harmony.
- Explains existence of suffering.
- Gives everyone clear guidelines for life.

2. KU
- Ahimsa or non-injury is non-killing.
- Non-injury is not merely non-killing.
- Ahimsa or non-injury means entire abstinence from causing any pain or harm whatsoever to any living creature, either by thought, word or deed.
- Non-injury requires a harmless mind, mouth and hand.
- It is the development of a mental attitude in which hatred is replaced by love.
- Ahimsa is true sacrifice.
- Ahimsa is forgiveness.
- Ahimsa is sakti (power).
- Ahimsa is true strength.

AE
Candidates will probably concentrate on ahimsa's importance but they are entitled to explore other aspects of Hindu belief which they consider more important than ahimsa.
Ahimsa has a role in:

Dharma:
which has as its central element – forgiveness, truthfulness, control of the mind, purity, practice of charity, control of the senses, non-violence, compassion, absence of greed and absence of malice as the ingredients of samanya. Dharma, the general law for all men – all of these are part of ahimsa.

Yoga:
Patanjali recommends that ten virtues should be practised by all men. The first five are: ahimsa (non-violence), satya (truthfulness), brahmacharya (celibacy in thought, word and deed), asteya (non-stealing) and aparigraha (non-covetousness). These constitute yama or self-restraint – all key features of ahimsa.

Gita:
fearlessness, purity of heart, steadfastness in the Yoga of Wisdom, self-restraint, straightforwardness, harmlessness, truth, absence of wrath, peacefulness, absence of crookedness, compassion to living beings, non-covetousness, mildness, vigour, forgiveness, purity and absence of envy and pride.

Margas:
Jnana involves control of the body and the senses, control of the mind, forbearance – again important in ahimsa. Bhakti aspirant must be spiritually and morally pure before embarking on the path and again principles of ahimsa are seen in here as with karma the path of selfless action where again moral virtue which embraces ahimsa is a key element.

Other aspects could be considered but these will be the main ones.

Section 4: Islam

1. *(a)*
- All of the prophets of the Old Testament.
- Jesus.
- Muhammad the last and final prophet.
- The angels of Allah.
- Messengers are those who deliver the word of Allah.

(b)
- The word of truth from Allah.
- Handed down directly through Muhammad.
- Teaches on all aspects of life.
- Offers guidance to all.
- The process of revelation.
- No need to seek help anywhere else.
- The source of all knowledge.
- Study of the Qur'an brings about a better person.

(c)
- Prayer is one of the Five Pillars.
- Relationship with Allah is maintained through prayer.
- Creates personal discipline via prayer five times per day.
- Good for the individual.
- Promotes the qualities of patience and virtue.
- Creates a sense of hope now and for the future.

1. (d) • Suffering is linked to death and is a fact of life, helps understanding.
   • Wrongdoing can lead to idolatry.
   • Suffering is a punishment for sin.
   • Suffering is a sign of the flawed nature of humanity.
   • It can be character building.
   • There will be less suffering if Muslims follow the will of Allah.
   • Suffering can lead to an awareness of the compassion of Allah.
   • Suffering is caused by selfishness.
   • The theory of instrumentality.
   • Necessary for the purpose of Allah.
   • Life is a time of testing.
   • Bring hope and comfort in times of grief.
   • Development of patience.

   (e) • State of barzakh between death and the day of judgement.
   • On the day of judgement all will be required to answer.
   • It is therefore a motivation to live a good life now.
   • Not only for the individual but for all nations.
   • Life in paradise is a reward for a good life.
   • Hell the result of disobedience.
   • This is a basic principle of Islam.
   • A fundamental and basic part of Islam.
   • Judgement in relation to Resurrection, Heaven and Hell.

2. KU
   • Final Pillar of Islam.
   • Human condition is a life of suffering.
   • Humans can be in a state of alienation to Allah due to the fall.
   • Alienation to each other/war etc.
   • Prayers to Allah at Mt Arafat.
   • Rejection of the devil at Mina.
   • Kissing of the black stone.
   • Helping to overcome the human condition.
   AE
   • Pilgrim becomes engrossed in the presence of Allah.
   • Shows man's subservience.
   • Worship through sacrifice.
   • Remembrance of the life of the prophet.
   • Humans lose all false ideas of the self.
   • Garments of ihram show equality of all beings.
   • Submit totally to the will of Allah in the rituals of hajj.
   • At the mercy of Allah.
   • Unique spiritual event.
   • Allah alone can aid them in the completion of hajj and thus overcome the human condition.
   • Could be said to help self awareness therefore bad.
   • Engender selfishness.
   • Equality for Muslims alone?
   • May make Muslims feel they are more important to Allah than others.
   • Other pillars may be more or less helpful in overcoming the human condition than hajj.

Section 5: Judaism

1. (a) • Man given sovereignty over nature.
   • God's nature: omniscient, omnipotent, omnipresent.
   • Creator, father, king, judge, teacher.
   • Human beings reflect God's nature.
   • Man has moral capacity, reason, free will.
   • Man can love God and have a spiritual bond.

   (b) • Cursed above all creatures.
   • Cursed ground.
   • Hard work.
   • Pain in childbirth.
   • Subject to man.
   • Dust to dust.

1. (c) • Moral conscience.
   • Instinct for survival.
   • Good when controlled.
   • Evil when uncontrolled.
   • Teachings of Torah provide control.

   (d) • Repentance (Teshuvah) offers a new beginning.
   • Returning to God.
   • Repentance is for sins against God.
   • Jews must make their own peace with fellow man.
   • Can repent at any time.
   • Rosh Hashanah and Yom Kippur - time for reflection.

   (e) • Greatest prophet was Moses.
   • Major prophets, eg Isaiah, Ezekiel, Jeremiah.
   • Role models of holiness and closeness to God.
   • Conveyed God's message to the people of Israel
   • Often their message was ignored – uncomfortable.
   • Criticised excessive luxury, idolatry, sexual immorality.
   • Called for justice and charity towards the poor and needy.
   • Foresaw and foretold consequences for the people.
   • Relevance of the prophets today.

2. Religious responsibilities eg:
   • Brit Milah, kashrut, bar/bat mitzvah, Shabbat, festivals, mezuzah/tefillin.

   Arguments about their importance:
   • obligations of Torah
   • taught to children from a young age
   • strengthen family life
   • develops identity and understanding of faith
   • brings about closeness to God
   • separates Jews from non-jewish culture
   • reform Judaism – many practices outdated and irrelevant.

Section 6: Sikhism

1. (a) • Guru refers to God in his role as Divine Teacher
   • 'True' emphasises the fact that, although prophets deliver God's message, God alone is the real source of their wisdom.

   (b) Description may include eg:
   • God's Will/Hukam is the active Force of Power that creates and controls all events and circumstances
   • God's will is beyond human understanding
   • God's Will can only be known by an act of revelation
   • Human beings make spiritual progress by learning to act in harmony with God's Will.

   (c) Relevant beliefs may include eg:
   • Sikhs believe that the Gurus were prophets chosen by God to reveal his Will
   • All Gurus shared the same soul/atma
   • Non-karmic births
   • Sikhs believe that the Gurus were reunited with God, their lives are therefore examples of totally God-centred lives.

   (d) Understanding may include eg:
   • Guru Granth Sahib was declared the Living Guru by the Tenth Guru, Guru Gobind Singh, before his death
   • Guru Gobind Singh said there would be no more human Gurus after him and that the Guru Granth Sahib was to be the only spiritual guide for Sikhs in the future.

**2007 Religious, Moral and Philosophical Studies
Higher Paper 2 (cont.)**

1. (d) (cont.)
Further explanation may include eg:
- not just a record of the Gurus' teachings but an active spiritual guide at all stages of life, just as the Gurus were while alive
- its words have the power to transform the lives of those who hear them (eg Sajjan the thief) just as the words of the Gurus did.

(e) Understanding may include eg:
- phrase refers to the belief that the soul/atma goes through many life-cycles (transmigration).
Further explanation may include eg:
- soul/atma may inhabit both animate and inanimate matter
- soul is part of God and will only find happiness/fulfilment when it reunites with God
- birth as a human is unique because it is only in human form that the soul can achieve reunion
- the soul's progress is determined by the law of karma which is part of the created order
- explanation of creation and effects of good and bad karma
- karma created by thoughts and actions
- once a person begins to act in harmony with God's Will all previous karma is erased and no new karma is created.

(f) Description of sewa and simran eg:
- Sewa as selfless service in a spirit of detachment
- examples of sewa in home, sangat, wider community
- Simran as constantly meditating on God and keeping the mind open to Him at all times
- examples of Simran eg Naam simran/japna, meditating on verse in Guru Granth.
Explanation of the benefits of both eg:
- through sewa, Sikhs are serving creating and therefore serving God
- serving others helps train the person to be less selfish
- selfishness is one of the greatest barriers to following God's Will
- through simran Sikhs keep the mind focused on God while serving Him through creation
- by keeping the mind focused on God Sikhs believe that they can avoid the temptations/evils which lead the soul away from God
- Simran helps the mind to understand God's Will which has been communicated through the words of the Gurus
- Sewa and simran are interlinked and of equal importance.

2. Any relevant description of maya and haumai eg:
- Maya, literally illusion
- does not imply that the physical world does not exist, only that we think it will last and stay the same
- the human tendency to treat physical objects/emotions/attachments as if they were lasting
- leads to soul away from God because it forgets that God is the only lasting part of reality
- Haumai is a result of maya
- means 'self-centredness'
- once human beings are under the spell of maya then all their actions become selfish because they have forgotten God.
In agreement with the statement:
- Maya and haumai are human tendencies which are part of God's created order so in that sense they cannot be avoided
- at all stages of spiritual development the soul can be overcome by maya and haumai eg becoming proud and self-satisfied because of deepening spiritual awareness/powers

2. (cont.)
- many Sikh practices seem to emphasise the importance of constantly trying to avoid these tendencies (eg sewa, simran, developing compassion, giving in charity, keeping the mind detached while living an active life in the world).
On the other hand:
- the Gurus taught that all will eventually be reunited with God therefore maya and haumai will be totally overcome at that point
- meditating on God at all times and selflessly serving others gradually train human beings to be less focused on their own desires and self
- becoming reunited with God happens during life, not after death and involves the state of sahej
- those who are reunited (jivan mukht) are unaffected by maya and haumai or any other temptation or physical sensation
- God's Grace can, at any time, help human beings overcome maya and haumai.

**2008 Religious, Moral and Philosophical Studies
Higher Specimen Question Paper
Paper 1**

SECTION 1: Morality in the Modern World

1. (a) A maximum of 2 marks for an account of the dilemma.

   Other points eg:
   - "piety", "pious or holy" refer to that which is morally "good"
   - It raises the question "What makes an action morally good?"
   - Socrates clearly implies actions are good in themselves.

   (b) Descriptions of eg:
   - Scripture as source of guidance
   - Tradition as source of guidance
   - Reason as source of guidance

2. (a) Description may include women as eg
   - subordinate
   - sex objects
   - virgin
   - mother
   - examples (television, advertising, film)

   (b) Examples may include eg:
   - scriptural teaching
   - scriptural interpretation
   - restrictive practices
   - historical examples
   - patriarchal religion
   - patriarchal

   (c) Examples from eg
   - legislation
   - media
   - education
   - employment
   - historic/contemporary comparison
   - assessment of success

   (d) Religious eg
   - divinely ordained role
   - God is above the secular
   - to change is to deny veracity of scripture/tradition
   - change not possible

   Moral eg
   - denies progress
   - dated morality
   - society has evolved
   - condones denial of rights
   - society shapes roles not God

3. (a) **Any 3 detailed points eg**
   - Revenge/ Deterrence/ Reformation/Protection
   - Society should feel that it has had some kind of revenge.
   - David has committed a crime and should be punished.
   - The punishment should deter others.
   - It needs therefore to be severe enough to deter both him and others.
   - It should bring about a change in the person.
   - It protects society from offenders.

   (b) Candidates may refer to the case study or to imprisonment in general eg

3. (b) continued

   Benefits eg
   - The person is off the street.
   - Society therefore feels safer and protected from his offending behaviour.
   - The crime figures in society may decrease during his incarceration.
   - He may end up in a prison that offers rehabilitation.
   - During his incarceration he will be able to begin to break his habit, this will be good for him and in the longer term for society.
   - He is being punished and he deserves so to be because of his offending.
   - He will suffer the consequences of his actions.

   Drawbacks eg
   - He may learn to become a better criminal while in prison.
   - He may leave prison with a grudge against society.
   - Society will have to pay for him and any dependants he has during his incarceration.

   (c) For example:
   - Fines – the person is asked to pay an appropriate monetary payment as a form of punishment.
   - Community service – The person will carry out a fixed amount of time working for and on behalf of the community.
   - Probation/rehabilitation – The judge may set a period of time for good behaviour with a course of rehabilitation.

   (d) Discussion may include eg:
   - Many religions would state that we should not harm therefore they would agree that reform is the only acceptable reason.
   - For example Buddhists would say that it is wrong to harm any living thing. Christianity would say turn the other cheek and love your enemies.
   - Retribution might be seen as selfish/selfishness is not acceptable from a religious stance.
   - Deterrence in fact does not deal with the root causes but merely creates a fear.
   - Some religious people might take the view that crime is not only an offence but a sin. Sin must be punished therefore cannot be morally wrong so to do.
   - Deterrence is in fact setting a good example and part of the learning process.
   - Utilitarians such as J S Mill would argue against the idea that punishment is only for reform.
   - That revenge/deterrence might lead to a safer society for the greater number of people.
   - Some might hold the view that the taking of a life which is very sacred/made in the image of God/cannot be treated by reform.
   - The concept of forgiveness suits reform rather than anything else.
   - Modern scientific theory supports the idea of reform.
   - The views of Philosophers studied on the views of punishment.
   - Groups/organisations such as the humanist society have views on punishment that would support and disagree with the statement.

4. (a) Description may include eg:
   - Legal but under strict criteria.
   - Doctor must be sure the request is voluntary and well-considered.

2008 Religious, Moral and Philosophical Studies
Higher Specimen Question Paper
Paper 1 (cont.)

4. (a) continued
   - Must be satisfied that suffering is unbearable and there is no chance of improvement.
   - Patient is fully aware of their situation and the prognosis.
   - Two thirds of requests are refused.
   - Doctors are not obliged to comply with requests for euthanasia.
   - A close doctor-patient relationship must be there – someone can't just go to Holland to request euthanasia.
   - Emphasis on dignity and relieving suffering.
   - All cases must be declared.

   (b) Explanation may include eg:
   - It is murder.
   - Goes against the laws of the land.
   - Goes against the laws of religion.
   - Undue emotional pressure on the person.
   - Respect for life.

   (c) Suggestions may include eg:
   - Makes it very clear that euthanasia is against the law.
   - Assisted suicide or voluntary euthanasia can result in a prison sentence of up to 14 years.
   - BMA has a clear policy opposing euthanasia.
   - It accepts that patients can refuse treatment that may prolong their lives and that medication designed to keep a patient pain-free and comfortable may reduce their life span.
   - It makes it clear that doctors may give large doses of drugs in order to keep a patient pain-free even if that means that it speeds up the person's death. However, it makes clear that they are not allowed to give out drugs with the intention of causing or speeding up death. This is called the doctrine of double effect.
   - BMA advice is effective in that it leaves the doctor and patient in no doubt about their rights.
   - It gives support ethically and legally.

   (d)
   - sanctity of life
   - God's gift
   - purpose to life
   - God's spirit within us
   - against religious teachings
   - how far should we let someone suffer?
   - or does suffering have real value?
   - can't be regulated safely
   - euthanasia is murder
   - slippery slope or wedge argument
   - euthanasia gives doctors too much power.
   - euthanasia may not be in the best interest of the patient.
   - good pain control makes euthanasia unnecessary
   - euthanasia sends the wrong message out about disability.
   - euthanasia may infringe upon other people's rights.

   Arguments in support of euthanasia:
   - euthanasia can be merciful
   - human beings have the right to die how and when they want to
   - the Libertarian argument.
   - euthanasia may be necessary for the fair distribution of resources.
   - euthanasia will always happen—so it would be better to regulate it properly.
   - it allows for a person to have their dignity.

5. (a) Any 3 relevant points eg
   - Bombs which unleash the power of nuclear fission or nuclear fusion eg atomic.
   - Warheads which contain chemicals that are highly damaging or fatal eg nerve agents.
   - Weapons which release agents that cause the spread of disease eg anthrax.

   (b) Any relevant points eg
   - WMD are indiscriminate in the damage they cause.
   - WMD are less easy to target.
   - WMD are more powerful and, therefore, likely to cause more devastation.
   - Conventional weapons are more predictable.

   (c) eg
   - Potential for massive destruction of human life
   - This includes civilian lives
   - Agonising deaths from radiation
   - Affects future generations eg genetically
   - Environmental damage

   (d)
   - Problems in enforcing the laws eg in some cases only a few nations sign treaty.
   - Although most weapons developed in the West, most wars fought in the developing world.
   - Most recent wars have been civil wars, rather than international
   - International law not recognised or ignored in certain parts of the world eg North Korea.
   - Various treaties on banning have been relatively successful, eg
     - proliferation (1968)
     - deploying nuclear weapons on the ocean floor (1971)
     - biochemical warfare (1975).
   - No nuclear bomb has been released since 1945.

   (e) Candidates must include two different viewpoints found in 1 or 2 religions eg
   - basis is fear, therefore, morally unacceptable
   - cannot lead to true peace
   - all energies focused on destructive not constructive development
   - references to religious leaders and/organisations/reports which have condemned this

   However,
   - moral duty to prevent war from ever occurring
   - duty to defend nation
   - moral duty to preserve certain beliefs and values eg justice, freedom, religion
   - non-action can be harmful
   - scriptural references which encourage preparing for war or defence

SECTION 2: Christianity: Belief and Science

   (a) A description of Aquinas' argument or alternative, eg
   - Ref to 1st cause argument of Aquinas.
   - Way 1 Change in the world/Way 2 Cause and Effect/Way 3 Being and non-Being/Way 4 degrees of Goodness and Perfection/Way 5 Order and Goals in Nature
   - All ways assume existence of God
   - "A posteriori" argument - based on observation
   - Heavy reliance on Aristotle's First Cause and Unmoved Mover 5

(b) A description of scientific method eg:
- Method summed up in the following:
  - observation
  - hypothesis
  - experiment
  - verification
- Basis of scientific method is empirical evidence
- Use of inductive reasoning
- Use of deductive reasoning
- 3 criteria for evaluating theory: agreement; internal relations; comprehensiveness
- scientific method affirms no theory can be proven.
- Coherency eg alternative theories

(c) Explanation may include eg:
- Scientists regard their theories as ultimately only a hypothesis and that it is always possible to refute them
- Science proceeds (Popper) not by induction but by deduction. According to Popper scientists begin with a theory (or conjecture), well informed queries that require to be experimentally tested, not to prove them true but to prove them false. When all have been shown to be false except one, it can be concluded that at least for the time being the remaining theory is the correct one.
- No theory is safe for all time and there are many examples of this: the Ptolemaic view of the universe was falsified by Copernicus; the physics of Newton was superseded by Einstein
- Scientists cannot be purely objective

(d) This question may draw on a wide choice of answer eg:
- Revelation means that God has taken the initiative in revealing something of his attributes to humans eg Moses on Mt Sinai; the supreme revelation of God in Christ
- Difference between general and special revelation - special is seen as an extension of religious experience
- Revelation of God through scripture - providing truth in all matters including history and science
- Revelation through the word
- Revelation through works of God - nature - God as designer and purposer

(e) Examples:
- Human reasoning and empirical observation are a much surer means of aiming at truth than theological doctrine and scriptural revelation
- Science is impartial. Scientists begin from a neutral standpoint and are not influenced by previous experience or future expectations
- Science is grounded in facts, proof and the principal of verification. Nothing is accepted as truth unless it can be verified
- Christian revelation is dependent on faith which is not as secure as reason in seeking truth

(f)
- Content of Genesis.1
- Name and describe Creationist standpoint
- Creationist standpoint - Science is wrong, Bible is right
- Literal interpretation of Genesis.1 must be accepted
- God made the universe the way it is and it hasn't changed

(f) continued

Analysis may include eg:
- Creationists insist on literal translation because Christianity is a **faith**. Proof is **not** required. Any other interpretation is lack of faith
- Creationists insist on veracity of whole bible – why doubt Genesis 1?
- Scientific evidence shows divine intervention – testing faith

(g) Candidates may consider the possibility of compatibility in their answer. They may disagree with the statement but in doing so may consider the alternatives.
- Religion and science are complementary - science asks How? religion asks Why?
- Big bang acceptable to many Christians because it allows a First Cause, Unmoved Mover theory as a cause of the Big Bang
- Steady state does not allow for a creator
- Some modern thinkers see Big Bang as giving us more understanding of the power of God. Size, complexity of the universe point to a Creator God
- Polkinghorne; Davies – identifying Designer/purposer behind the Big Bang
- Mary Midgely - 2 maps of reality. (Do the contours of both maps fit? As most obvious criticism)
- God First Cause - guarantor of physical and mathematical laws
- Recent revival of interest in Natural Theology
- Genesis and Big Bang both true. Full understanding beyond humans. Only God can fully comprehend
- Anthropic Principle Fine-tuning of universe dependent on mind behind it
- Creationist and Atheistic arguments to contradict all of the above

**2008 Religious, Moral and Philosophical Studies
Higher Specimen Question Paper
Paper 2**

SECTION 1: BUDDHISM

1. (a) Anicca:
    - impermanence
    - nothing lasts forever
    - everything physical, emotional etc is constantly changing

    Dukkha:
    - unsatisfactoriness
    - attachment to impermanent things leads to suffering when things change

    (b) (1) Body or material form (rupa)
    Matter has 4 elements: solidity, fluidity, heat, motion. These are experienced through our sense organs. Physical form is always changing and is dependent on its environment for its continued existence.
    (2) Feeling or sensations (vedana)
    Arise from contact between sense organ and sense object. Can be pleasant, unpleasant, neutral.
    (3) Perceptions or mental processes (sanna)
    The ideas encountered by the mind. We recognise an object and see something as distinct from other things.
    (4) Impulses or constructing activities (sankharas)
    Willed activities of the mind. Mental formations. Responses to perceptions.
    (5) Consciousness (vinnana)
    Interpretation (misinterpretation) of things and events. Attaching value to things. Projection of our version of things on to what's there.

    (c) A description of the cycle of samsara eg
    - Cycle of rebirth
    - State of dependent origination
    - Rebirth depends on previous kamma
    - Links all beings in a web of existence
    - Flow of ever changing consciousness
    - Aim is to live life in such a way as to secure better Samsaric rebirth and get closer to escaping samsara

    (d) Points may include eg
    - Attachment to notion of "self" links to craving
    - Craving to put self at centre arises from ignorance
    - Ignorance is barrier to spiritual progress
    - Accepting anatta promotes unselfishness
    - Unselfishness seeks good for world rather than for individual
    - Will be trapped in samsara and in "house of life and death" until we realise anatta

    (e) Points may include eg
    - Human condition is one of suffering caused by not realising anatta and anicca
    - Putting self at centre is central to that suffering
    - Because there is no self to be centre, we will always suffer if we are full of ego
    - However, anatta has to be understood in relation to other marks of existence to make complete sense
    - Anatta, anicca and dukkha are interconnected
    - Anatta is simply anicca applied to people
    - Anicca is concept of impermanence of all things so Anatta is based on anicca
    - Dukkha is caused by tanha/craving for pleasures for self

1. (f) Points for KU may include eg:
    - Tanha is craving. 2nd Noble Truth
    - Fundamental cause of suffering.

    Points for AE may include eg:
    - Impermanence causes the fever of craving because we attempt to find satisfaction in a constantly changing world
    - Tanha attempts to "hold on" to object as well as crave object
    - But this is a hopeless task and leads to suffering
    - Must get rid of tanha to find happiness

2. Content of KU may include eg:
    - Meditation trains the mind and helps us to recognize our true nature.
    - Untrained minds need meditation to lead to purity and overcome ignorance.
    - Meditation eliminates cravings and illusion of self.
    - Liberation is hindered by untrained mind.
    - Meditation helps overcome problems of the Human Condition.
    - Calms the restless activity of "self".
    - Helps compassion arise. Attachment ceases.
    - Samatha meditation calms the mind and increases self-awareness and self-harmony.
    - Vipassana gives insight to true reality.

    Content of AE may include eg:
    Reasons why Buddhists would agree that meditation is vital for enlightenment may include:
    - The Buddha achieved enlightenment through meditation.
    - Meditation is journey towards liberation from the self.
    - Meditation is basic to the dhamma.
    - Mental discipline has to be practised alongside wisdom and ethical conduct to achieve nibbana.

    Reasons why it could be argued that meditation is not the main key to enlightenment, and that other aspects of Buddhist practice are also important may include:
    - The fact that meditation is practised alongside ethical conduct and wisdom in the Eightfold Path shows that they are of equal importance.
    - Practise of morality decreases suffering of others and of ourselves, so we gain self-harmony from that.
    - We purify ourselves through morality – the antidote to dukkha.
    - Mental discipline without ethical conduct is empty.
    - Wisdom is also required to understand the Human Condition, so the study of scriptures is also a key to self-harmony.

SECTION 2: CHRISTIANITY

1. (a)
    - God Incarnate—God takes on human flesh.
    - Human with all the potential and possible frailties of humanity.
    - Son of God/Virgin Birth

    (b) Description may include, eg:
    - by feeding the hungry
    - by looking after the poor
    - by giving drink to those who are thirsty
    - by visiting those in prison
    - by caring for the sick

1. (c) Explanation may include eg:
   - Worship helps to build and strengthen the community of Christians.
   - Prayer within worship strengthens relationship with God.
   - Eucharist meal builds up the fellowship of the church.
   - The worshippers will learn about the teachings of Jesus.
   - They will become aware of the demands of these teachings to care for others.
   - They will in the Eucharist/mass and by study learn the importance of loving neighbour as self.
   - A description of the Christian understanding of Kingdom of God. Heaven/Earth.

   (d) Explanation of eg:
   - Life after death with God
   - Spiritual life in the Holy Spirit
   - Life in all its fullness
   - A new view of the world
   - Belief in the certainty of a future life
   - Restored relationship with God
   - Description of heaven/hell

   (e) Points may include, eg:
   - Jesus is owed service and loyalty
   - Worshipped like a king
   - Loves and is loved by subjects
   - Judges
   - Provides security for His subjects

2.
   - God raises Jesus from the dead confirming his life
   - God will save humankind by overcoming death
   - It shows that Jesus has defeated death
   - Christians have the promise of eternal life
   - Had Jesus not risen there would be no salvation and no hope
   - Resurrection gives new meaning to Jesus' life for Christians
   - Salvation for all believers
   - Fear is removed from death
   - Christ is a constant strength and presence
   - It gives a focus to the Christian faith
   - The Christian church exists because of resurrection of Jesus

   Candidates may discuss the historicity of the resurrection.
   - Not a physical event but a spiritual one.
   - Belief in the event but not the importance.
   - It has been said it was mass illusion so not a ground for faith.
   - Incarnation could be seen to be more important.
   - A plot by the Romans therefore again not central to the faith of believers.
   - Baptism of believers more important.

SECTION 3: HINDUISM

1. (a) Ignorance of eg:
   - True nature of self
   - Brahman
   - Universe
   - True nature of reality 3

   (b) Points may include eg:
   - Ignorant of true nature
   - Book knowledge not experienced knowledge
   - Pass on false teachings
   - Do not see the truth
   - Leading the lost further into the depths of ignorance
   - Knowledge freely given by God.

1. (c) KU is a description of concepts. AE is an explanation of how they relate to avidya.
   - Avidya as it relates to samsara
   - Dukkha
   - Desire
   - Maya
   - Brahman
   - Atman

   (d) A description of dharma may include, eg:
   - Importance of doing own dharma
   - Varna dharmas divinely ordained
   - Description of varna dharmas
   - Description of ashramas
   - Vedic teachings

   (e) KU involves, eg:
   - Identification of "atman" as "soul" or part of "enduring reality"

   AE involves, eg:
   - Explanation of dualistic understandings of the atman
   - Explanation of non-dualistic understanding of the atman

2. Discussion may include, eg:
   - Description of the 3 margas
   - Associated practices
   - The 4 varnas
   - Acknowledgement and understanding of the variety of practice within Hinduism

SECTION 4: ISLAM

1. (a) Description may include, eg:
   - Alienation from God
   - Alienation from each other
   - Alienation from humanity
   - Alienation from creation
   - Pain in childbirth
   - Death

   (b) Description may include, eg:
   - Each person is free to choose his/her own actions
   - They may choose to act in accordance with the will of Allah
   - Repentance is a real possibility if the person is sincere
   - Although each person's life is predestined each person is free to choose how they live their lives

   (c) Explanation may include:
   - Suffering linked to death; a fact of life
   - Wrongdoing leads to suffering–human nature is flawed
   - Wrongdoing can lead to idolatry
   - Suffering is a punishment for sin
   - Suffering can be character building
   - Muslims will suffer less if they stop questioning the will of Allah
   - Suffering is contained within the omnipotence of Allah
   - Through suffering people become aware of the compassion of Allah
   - Life is a test, suffering is part of the process
   - Suffering comes through indifference to the needs of others
   - Theory of instrumentality—suffering is necessary for the purpose of Allah
   - Comparison with suffering after death and in Hell

2008 Religious, Moral and Philosophical Studies
Higher Specimen Question Paper
Paper 2 (cont.)

(d) • State of Barzakh between death and The Day of Judgement
   • There will be a great day when all will stand before Allah and answer for their actions
   • Not only does each individual have its book of deeds but each nation
   • Each nation will have to answer to Allah
   • Life in paradise for those who have a preponderance of good
   • Life in hell for those who have a preponderance of evil
   • This belief in life after death and a new life after judgement is a basic principle in Islam
   • All of the above show the great importance of this belief for all Muslims

(e) KU may include, eg:
   • What the Qur'an is
   • What is in the Qur'an
   • How it was revealed

   Explanation may include, eg:
   • The centrality of the Qur'an
   • The unchangeable word of Allah
   • Passed on through Muhammad the last and greatest prophet of Allah
   • Teaching for all aspects of life
   • Teaches how to submit to Allah

2. Discussion may include, eg:
   • Third pillar of Islam
   • Paid at the end of every lunar year
   • How this is divided
   • In Sunni paid to the state
   • Shias pay to their mujtahid
   • Categories of people to whom it is paid
   • Link between performance and the laying of a foundation to faith
   • Submission and worship through action
   • Zakat serves humans but also shows worship to Allah
   • Heart of the recipient is purified from jealousy
   • Overcomes selfishness
   • Benevolence is a principle of Islam
   • Source of blessing to the individual
   • Zakat follows the example of the prophet
   • Wealth can be a stumbling block between humans and Allah
   • Zakat is a part of worship–Ibadah
   • Shows total submission to Allah which leads to mercy
   • Allah alone can provide the means to overcome the problems of the human condition but zakat plays an important part
   • Shows awareness of belonging to umma

But it could be said that eg:
   • Prayer is much more helpful
   • Submission to Allah is more than just zakat
   • Following the teachings of Muhammad and Qur'an is more important
   • Taking part in hajj as a one-off event may be more life-changing

SECTION 5: JUDAISM

1. (a) Description may include eg:
   • Jewish people slaves in Egypt for hundreds of years
   • Moses returned from exile to lead his people
   • 10 plagues

(b) Describe the terms of the Covenant, eg
   • God's protection and reward for obedience
   • Bring the Jews into their promised land
   • Obedience to the commands of God

   Explain importance, eg
   • Still relevant to Jews today
   • Obligations of Covenant define and influence Jewish lifestyle
   • Origin of Torah and Oral Tradition

(c) Description may include eg:
   • Every week on the seventh day
   • Friday sunset to Saturday sunset
   • Ends with Havdalah
   • Observes the 4th commandment
   • Follows God's example at creation
   • Different from other days
   • No work (39 melachot)
   • Special preparations, blessings
   • Synagogue worship

(d) • Care for the weak, orphans and widows
   • Giving of charity
   • Regard for rights of others
   • Golden Rule
   • Importance of justice
   • Helps control Yetzer Harah

(e) Three laws might come from—Kashrut, festivals, Brit Milah or any other appropriate area.

   Evaluation may include eg:
   • Practical problems in obeying the laws, eg access to kosher food, having to work on festival days etc
   • Problems associated with prejudice and discrimination
   • Ethical issues, eg rights of the child in Brit Milah
   • More difficult in some areas/countries than other

2. KU may include eg:
   • Man given free will
   • Man is responsible for actions
   • Genesis 3—disobedience
   • Consequence of sin is further evil
   • Yetzer Tov and Yetzer Harah

   AE may include eg:
   • sMuch suffering is inexplicable
   • Moral failure is a theme running through Torah—prophets
   • Torah study and observance aims at controlling Yetzer Harah
   • Acknowledgement of human responsibility leads to moral and social behaviour
   • Explanation of suffering as punishment for disobedience difficult to accept

SECTION 6: SIKHISM

1. (a) Two relevant points eg
   - Guru refers to God in His role as Divine Teacher
   - "True" emphasises the fact that, although prophets (eg 10 Gurus) teach God's message, God alone is the real source of this wisdom

   (b) Description may include eg:
   - Kam—(lust) sexual promiscuity/excess and any sexual conduct outwith heterosexual marriage
   - Krodh—(anger) unjustified and controlled anger against another person
   - Lobh—(greed) excessive desire for material wealth/physical gain
   - Moh—(excessive attachment to worldly "things") excessive love for, or reliance on, human beings/material success for satisfaction in life
   - Ankhar—(pride) regarded as worst of "evils". Mentally taking personal credit for the successes freely given by God

   (c) Any relevant description of Nam Simran eg:
   - It is the practice of remembering God at all times
   - Verbal or mental repetition of "Sat Nam/Waheguru" (eg)
   - Meditation beads may also be used

   Explanation may include eg:
   - Ultimate aim of life is to merge with God
   - Aim can only be achieved by constantly turning the soul's attention to God
   - By keeping mind focused on/open to God may be more ready to receive God's Grace
   - May be less likely to fall prey to maya or become self-centred (haumai)

   (d) KU may include eg:
   - Someone who is total human or self-centred
   - May contain a contrast with Gurmukh
   - May give an example of the type of person who is Manmukh

   AE may include eg:
   - Manmukh has become a slave to maya (illusion of permanence)
   - Reason for this is ego (haumai)
   - If Manmukh remains in this state will waste the opportunity to merge with God and re-enter cycle of transmigration
   - Being human offers a rare opportunity which may not reoccur for many lifetimes

   (e) KU may include eg:
   - Merging with God
   - Involves reunion of the soul with its original source
   - Phrase "Obtains the name"
   - Can only ultimately be achieved by Grace of God

   AE may include eg:
   - Human beings can "help themselves" by service and prayer (sewa, simran)
   - "contemplating", "meditating"
   - Reunion with God not after death—Jiran Mukhti
   - State of bliss ("enraptured")—when all material and worldly concerns are irrelevant ("carefree . . . doubt eradicated")

2. Any accurate description of Sikh understanding of "equality" eg
   - All people are equal irrespective of race, religion etc
   - Based on belief that atma is part of God
   - Of central importance to Sikh faith
   - First teaching of Guru Nanak

   In agreement eg:
   - Doesn't always work in practice—culture and religious faith may become confused (eg women only being allowed menial "sewa" in Gurdwara or equivalent example)
   - Many practices associated with equality make sense in Punjab/India but not Scotland eg sitting on floor as a sign of equality (what about old or disabled?)
   - Individual Gurdwaras are sometimes associated with 1 caste

   In disagreement eg:
   - Many Sikh practices (eg sitting/eating together, all allowed to lead worship) help reinforce idea of equality
   - This gives clear sense of the value to each individual in own right
   - All can participate equally and gain real sense of community/belonging
   - Fits with modern idea of "equality"
   - Candidates may include examples where Sikhs have recognised practices which go against teachings regarding equality and have protested/petitioned for reform.

2008 Religious, Moral and Philosophical Studies Higher Paper 1

Section 1 – Morality in the Modern World

1. (a)
   - Religious writings are central to all religions.
   - They contain rules and guidelines regarding ethical behaviour.
   - Ethical behaviour is tied in to outcome in afterlife, eg Judaism:
   - Torah contains law. 613 mitzvoth. Rules for moral living.
   - Purpose is to keep covenant with God and to make world perfect again.
   - Obedience brings Jews closer to God.

   (b)
   - Kantian ethics – for Kant the key issue is how to discover a rational basis for ethics.
   - The Categorical imperative is a priori – we can see that it is true without having to experience it.
   - Define categorical imperative – act only on that maxim whereby you can at the same time will that it should become a universal law.
   - The Categorical Imperative is a principle of pure practical reason.
   - Moral actions are done from a sense of duty.
   - A moral person is one who acts from a sense of duty not from inclination.
   - Acting morally amounts to doing one's duty whatever consequences might follow.
   - Motive of an action is more important than the action and its consequences.

   (c)
   - Utilitarianism: actions are good or bad depending on the outcome.
   - The moral consequences of the action is the promotion of human happiness/well being and the minimising of unhappiness/pain.
   - The aim is to achieve consequences that will bring about the greatest happiness for the greatest number of people – Utilitarainism.
   - Distinction between act-utilitarianism and rule utilitarianism.
   - Reference to Mill or Bentham's position.

Gender

2. (a)
   - Equal pay for equal job.
   - Employee's rights/Employers' Responsibilities.
   - Tax and inheritance laws.
   - Equality in employment.

   (b)
   - Equal pay now an expectation and a right, not a hope.
   - Some traditional stereotypes and attitudes still exist.
   - Wage gap still exists and increases with age.
   - Prevalence of part-time work.
   - Women's work less valued.
   - Equal pay in principle but hidden differences, eg overtime.

   (c)
   - Outline UN statements (eg CEDAW).
   - Explicitly calls for economic justice as a human right.
   - Vision for fairer more equal world.
   - Raises public awareness of issues.
   - Calls for equal contribution and participation of women on equal terms with men.

2. (d)
   - Different interpretations of scripture.
   - Teachings of different founders/leaders.
   - Influence of leading devotees and/or organisations within the religion.
   - Different traditions expressing a variety of views.
   - Weighting given to scripture, tradition, contemporary views.
   - Place of individual conscience in decision-making.
   - Historical/cultural development of a religion.

   (e) Reference should be made to sources (moral philosophers and organisations) which are independent of religious belief, eg
   - Utilitarian moral principles.
   - EOC guidelines.
   - Humanist briefings.
   - Beijing platform.
   - Examples of economic injustice and discrimination.
   - Social benefits of equality.
   - Economic equality as a human right.
   - Implications for traditional male/female roles.

Crime and Punishment

3. (a)
   - It could be argued it was a deterrent to others.
   - It is less costly than life imprisonment.
   - The community might feel safer that such a criminal will never be free again.
   - Justice is seen to be done.
   - It is the most fitting form of punishment for murder.

   (b)
   - They might argue that it is a form of torture.
   - That it deprives people of any respect at all.
   - Nobody has the right to take the life of another.
   - Governments become murderers.
   - It is degrading.

   (c)
   - It could be argued that one is less humiliating than another.
   - All forms are morally wrong.
   - Argue from the process of execution that one is more moral than another.
   - Refer to the United Nations Declaration.
   - Argument for and against CP might be included.
   - The end result is the taking of a life therefore wrong.
   - Utilitarian arguments could be used.
   - Religious viewpoints expressed.
   - 2 marks can be gained for describing 2 forms of execution.

   (d)
   - There was considerable amount of public unrest.
   - Protests held outside the prison made the government uncomfortable.
   - Became a landmark in changing the views of many people.
   - Questions about the execution of one with learning difficulties.
   - The fact that later new evidence came to light but it was too late for Evans.
   - It was shown later that police evidence was unreliable but again too late to change events.
   - Evidence later showed he was wrongly convicted (pardoned)
   - 2 marks can be gained for facts about the Timothy Evans case.

3. (*e*)
- It might be a benefit to society making people feel safer.
- Murderers have gone against the will of God.
- God gives life and only God can take it away.
- An Eye for an Eye.
- Right Livelihood means that you cannot harm another not even a murderer.
- It is a better punishment than a life in prison which removes the dignity given to humanity by God.
- It would save a great deal of money that could be used to help the poor, religious people would approve of this use of money.
- Jesus instructs us to love our enemies.
- Judgement belongs to God.
- It serves the greater good.
- More happiness by the death of one, religious groups seek happiness for all.
- Arguments put forward by specific groups within religion ie The Quakers opposed.
- Capital punishment could be seen as less cruel to the criminal than a long term of deprivation.
- The use of appropriate scriptural quotations should be awarded.

Medical Ethics

4. (*a*)
- Changing the genetic makeup of cells or tissues.
- Modifying the building blocks that carry our hereditary material.
- May involve somatic gene therapy ie alteration of gene deficiencies.
- May involve germline gene therapy ie alteration in sperm or egg which persists to successive generations.
- May involve cloning of embryos for reproduction or harvesting stem cells.

(*b*)
- Embryos up to 14 days old may be used under licence.
- Allows experimentation on in vitro embryos for therapeutic purposes.
- As well as the disposal of surplus embryos including those used for experimentation.
- Embryos can be stored for up to 5 years.
- Allows cloning of embryos under licence for therapeutic purposes.

(*c*)
- Embryos used to harvest stem cells destroyed.
- Some groups consider embryos as human life ie persons.
- Should one life be taken to save another?
- If regarded as persons, should embryos be used as a means to an end?
- Cloned embryos used in UK when UN resolution against this.
- Human life will be treated as a commodity.

(*d*) Teachings on eg
- Instructions to heal.
- Alleviation of suffering.
- Compassion.
- The Golden Rule.
- Human responsibility/stewardship, etc.
- Co-creators, vice-gerents, etc.
- Duty to develop knowledge, creativity, etc.

(*e*) KU: Maximum of 3 marks for information on cloning
- Producing an organism that is a genetic copy of another.
- May apply to cells, not just complete organism.
- Human Reproductive Cloning Act 2001 forbids human cloning for reproductive purposes.
- HFEA allows human cloning for therapeutic purposes.

AE
Arguments supporting statement eg
- Erosion of value and dignity of human life.
- Individual life becomes a commodity or a manufactured object.
- UN Declaration on Human Genome and Human Rights says it is contrary to human dignity.
- Cloning is asexual, therefore, against nature.
- Parentage and family relationships distorted.
- Clone a means to an end, not an end in itself.
- Substantial risks of unpredictable debilitating and lethal conditions.
- Used to create 'designer babies'.
- Psychological/social harm because of expectations and stigma.
- Only open to a small group of wealthy people.
- Drain on health resources.

Arguments opposing statement eg
- Most people do not accept absolutes in morality.
- Every scientific advance can be put to good use in some situation.
- Offers a new treatment option for infertile couples.
- Offers hope of a healthy child to couples who are genetically at risk.
- Offers an opportunity to select desirable traits.
- Could improve the human race.
- People should be free to make own reproductive decisions.
- Can't disinvent it, only hope to control it.
- Part of fundamental right to have and raise children.

War and Peace

5. (*a*) **Pacifists**
- Opposed to war.
- Believes that conflict and war can be solved by non-violent means.
- Refusal to participate in military action.

Christian Pacifist/Conscientious Objector
- Teaching of Jesus – non-violence, justice – only way to true peace.
- "Turn the other cheek".
- Conscience guided by God – God would never allow war.

Humanist/Pragmatic
- One life – use it to the full.
- Protect future generations.
- Violence breeds violence.
- Generally against war – but may choose to fight if the threat is greater than not fighting eg WW II.

(*b*)
- To save future generations from war.
- Reaffirm fundamental Human Rights.
- Establish conditions under which justice and respect can be maintained.
- Practice tolerance and live in peace.
- Maintain international peace.

(*c*)
- Believe in Humans – only 1 life.
- Make the best of this life.
- Life is special and should be nurtured.
- Believe it is up to humans to decide what is right and what is wrong.
- Generally anti-war – we do not have the right to inflict suffering on others.
- Golden Rule.

2008 Religious, Moral and Philosophical Studies Higher Paper 1 (cont.)

5. (c) continued

- Some may, however, agree to fight because the threat is too great to ignore but as innocent people will lose their lives this raises a moral question.
- The result of not fighting might be worse than fighting.

(d) **Some may believe**

- That it is their moral duty to defend nation.
- Just War.
- Duty to defend certain beliefs and values eg justice, freedom and religion.
- Lesser of two evils.
- Use of Biblical material – Romans 13:5.
- Biblical material encouraging preparation for war.
- Non-action could do more damage.

On the other hand

- Jesus taught that violence is wrong.
- War causes fear which is morally unacceptable.
- "Sermon on the Mount" – Blessed are the Peace Makers.
- Ahimsa – non harmfulness.

(e) **In favour of the statement**

- Nations have a duty to defend themselves.
- Raises moral implications when you have to watch innocent people suffering and dying due to oppression.
- To sit back and let whole communities be destroyed by chemical or biological weapons is a crime against humanity.
- Situation Ethics – violence may have to be used if it results in the greater good in the long run.

Against the statement

- Pacifists believe that non-violence is the true way to justice, freedom and equality.
- Violence only breeds more violence.
- Pacifism is a complex process involving negotiation, the promoting of peace and peace-making.
- Plenty of evidence of successful pacifist action.
- The effect of non-conventional weapons is too great to contemplate – loss of life of combatants and non-combatants – environmental damage – economic problems. Use of these weapons should not be conscienced.

SECTION 2: CHRISTIANITY: BELIEF AND SCIENCE

(a)   maximum of 2 marks for description of Big Bang
- Heat.
- Redshift of galaxies.
- Microwave background radiation.
- Primordial elements.
- Spread and distribution of galaxies.
- Inflation.

(b)
- Christian understanding of God's role in creation
- Literal
- Part literal/part myth.
- Myth.
- Candidates may give examples of understandings.

(c)
- Aquinas proposed it.
- Everything has a cause.
- Nothing exists by itself.
- Can't have an infinite regression of causes.
- Must be a first cause.
- Must be an uncaused cause.
- Uncaused cause is God.
- Or any alternative to Aquinas eg Kalam argument.

(d)
- Big Bang suggests a beginning.
- No pre-existing matter.
- Something cannot come out of nothing.
- Something had to cause Big Bang.
- Cause was God.

(e)
- Not in the Bible.
- Bible version is true, science is wrong.
- Big Bang has limitations.
- There are other theories.
- Denies that God is creator.
- Denies that God is the designer.
- Removes God from the process of creation.
- Removes purpose from creation.

(f)   maximum of 2 marks for description of scientific method in relation to its limitations
- Only asks how questions, not why questions.
- Can only deal with the empirical.
- Guesswork plays a part in scientific method.
- Scientists disagree.
- Science has been wrong in the past.
- Paradigms change.

(g)   maximum of 2 marks for description of revelation in relation to its limitations
- Based on faith.
- Not factual.
- Contradictory.
- Not based on empirical observation.
- Range of interpretations.
- Matter of opinion.

(h) **KU**
- Random mutation.
- Element of chance.
- Natural selection.
- Synthesis of genetics and natural selection.
- Universe is complex.
- Too complex to be chance.
- Complexity requires a designer.
- Paley's analogy.

AE
- Creationist response – strengths and weaknesses.
- Conservative response – strengths and weaknesses.
- Intelligent Design – strengths and weaknesses.
- Evolutionary Theism – strengths and weaknesses.
- Anthropic Principle in its various forms.

2008 Religious, Moral and Philosophical Studies
Higher Paper 2

SECTION 1: BUDDHISM

1. (a)
   - Dhamma there waiting to be discovered for each universe.
   - Siddhartha meditated under Bo tree until he discovered it at his enlightenment.
   - Told it to 5 ascetics at deer park in Benares – turning wheel of Dhamma.
   - Travelled rest of life sharing Dhamma.

   (b)
   - Literally means actions.
   - Natural law of cause and effect.
   - Results of our actions are visited upon us at a future time – either immediately, later in this life or in future lifetime.
   - Doesn't come back in same form.
   - Impossible to trace back web of actions.
   - "unskilful" actions bind unenlightened to Samsara.
   - "skilful" actions lead towards enlightenment.

   (c)
   - Anything that would keep them on Samsara.
   - 3 poisons – greed sourced in desires, so won't escape Samsara
     hatred leads to bad kamma
     ignorance of Buddhist way does not allow progress to Nibbana.
   - Bad kamma which keeps them on Samsara.

   (d)
   - Knowing faults leads to taking action to put them right.
   - The treasure is the goal of Nibbana that can be achieved if you realise faults and try to remedy them.
   - MUST sort out faults to reach Nibbana.

   (e)
   - Don't believe in God, so there is no being to please by following it – don't get enlightenment "by god's grace" – only reach enlightenment by following Dhamma.
   - Each individual has to follow OWN path to perfection and it is the Dhamma that shows the way they have to follow.
   - Dhamma can be abandoned once enlightenment has been found, so it is only a vehicle for reaching goal through their own effort.

   (f) KU might include
   - Sangha is body of monks established by Buddha as group who received Dhamma.
   - Early Sangha kept Dhamma pure by passing it on.
   - Still has function in passing on Dhamma in teaching others etc.
   - Key role in Theravadin Buddhism.

   AE might include
   Is Sangha central?
   Yes
   - Without it there would be no purity of teachings.
   - Without it, no point in Buddha revealing Dhamma.
   - Monastic Sangha facilitates following of Dhamma.
   - Arya Sangha inspiration as perfect example.

   No
   - All three jewels equally important.
   - Could claim Dhamma most important as, without it, the understanding of the way would not exist.
   - Sangha would have no purpose without Dhamma.
   - None of this would have existed without Buddha.

2.
   - Arhat is holy man or saint
   - always male
   - achieves enlightenment enters parinibbana
   - doesn't have rebirth
   - Bodhisattva is on verge of attaining Nibbana
   - puts off final Nibbana to return to teach others to save from suffering.

   Reasons why Arhat is true ideal:
   - it is the ideal for Theravadins
   - way of elders, so the practice is closest to way preached by Gautama himself
   - gives examples to others, so is effective
   - has wisdom, morality, skill in meditation, detachment, so clearly works and has skill to help others
   - teaches others to allow them to progress, just like Buddha
   - allows laity to provide for him…to let them gain karma.

   Reasons why Bodhisattva is ideal:
   - Mahayana ideal
   - gives ordinary Buddhists a meaningful spiritual life…arhat too difficult for most
   - shows active and ultimate compassion for others by delaying Nibbana…unlike arhat…so more in keeping with aims of Buddhism
   - easier to reach enlightenment than in Theravadin.

SECTION 2: CHRISTIANITY

1. (a) **Any two relevant points eg**
   - All people who have faith in God.
   - Those who have inherited the faith of Abraham.
   - Background details of Abraham's faith from Genesis.
   - Those made righteous not because of actions but faith.

   (b) maximum of 2 KU marks for defining Incarnation
   - Jesus is God Incarnate.
   - He was both fully God and fully man.
   - Born of woman and Holy Spirit.
   - Existing in the beginning.

   Important because eg
   - Only a human being could understand our condition.
   - Or pay for our sin.
   - Only way we could understand the nature of God.
   - Role model/ideal human for Christians to imitate.

   (c)
   - Teachings.
   - Humanity.
   - Mission
     eg from his life and teaching
     eg from the teaching and tradition of the church.

   (d)
   - Results of human disobedience.
   - The Fall.
   - Misuse of freewill.
   - Creation spoiled.
   - Result of alienation from God.
   - Alienation from each other.
   - And alienation from the rest of creation.

   (e) maximum of 2 KU marks for descriptions of prayer or meditation
   - Thanking, adoring, conferring with, petitioning God.

2008 Religious, Moral and Philosophical Studies Higher Paper 2 (cont.)

1. (*e*) continued

- Still, quiet time of focus, concentration on spiritual matters.
- Found in solitary or collective worship.

Helps to eg
- Deepen relationships with God through adoration.
- Through listening more carefully to his instructions.
- Through experiencing his presence and forgiveness.
- Deepen relationship with our neighbour through connecting with common humanity.
- Through ridding ourselves of negative thoughts.
- Through strengthening conviction.

(*f*)
- Not all suffering seems to have a purpose.
- Not all suffering seems to be caused by human sin.
- If God is sovereign, then he is responsible for suffering.
- If God is both good and omnipotent, why doesn't he stop innocent suffering?
- Either he is limited in power or in goodness.

2. (*a*)
- Betrayed by Judas, his own disciple.
- Tried unjustly in various courts.
- Beaten and mocked by Roman soldiers.
- Crucified between two thieves, outside city walls.
- Died a criminal's death after 6 hours of torture and taunting.

(*b*) **Very important because through Jesus' suffering and death, Christians believe.**
- We are released from the human condition of sin, guilt and death.
- The broken relationship between God and humanity is restored.
- We are justified, if we believe.
- We are redeemed – a ransom has been paid.
- Jesus took place of humanity.
- A sacrificial offering has been made to atone for sin.
- Jesus exemplifies the perfect life, demonstrating God's love that makes sinners repent.
- God overcomes the cosmic powers of evil.

However, other aspects also very important eg
- Incarnation – salvation depends on Jesus' humanity and divinity.
- Holy Spirit's work within, new creation.
- Faith is dead without works – moral wholeness.
- Jesus' life and example of complete obedience to God.
- Resurrection guarantees eternal life.
- Some believe salvation is also social/political.

SECTION 3: HINDUISM

1. (*a*)
- Sruti – revelation direct from God.
- Contains Krishna's revelation to Arjuna.
- Explains what God is like.
- Explains the importance of the margas.
- Explains caste and dharma.
- Contains main tenets of Hinduism.
- Has a role in rites of passage and worship.

1. (*b*)
- Student – study and learning.
- Householder – family, work and community.
- Forest dweller – greater contemplation and limited withdrawal.
- Wanderer – renunciation, teaching.

(*c*)
- It is the cosmic order.
- Gives everything a purpose.
- Gives everything a role.
- Promotes social cohesion.
- Governs morality.
- Governs social structure.
- Decreed by Brahman.
- Key role in karma, samsara and moksha.

(*d*)
- Karma determines varna.
- Good karma means good varna.
- Bad karma means bad varna.
- Karma encourages acceptance of varna.
- Karma encourages fulfilment of varna dharma.
- Performance of varna dharma is good karma.

(*e*)
- System is abused.
- Advantages upper caste.
- Treatment of dalits.
- Rules are not scriptural.
- Discriminatory.
- Form of apartheid.
- Denies human rights.
- Promotes inequality.
- Cannot change it.
- Cannot help the caste you are in.
- Caste system has allowed invaders to enter India.
- Divides society.

(*f*)
- It is in Vedas.
- Rules made up by men not God.
- Karma dictates caste.
- Gives everyone a role.
- It is honest – class discrimination exists everywhere, no pretence of natural equality.
- Present caste is for one life only.
- Remove caste and Hindu society breaks down.
- Caste system has held India together.
- Gives an aim in life.
- Promotes co-operation in society.

2. **KU – descriptions of**
- Transience.
- Avidya.
- Nature of Brahman.
- Nature of reality.
- Gunas.
- Samsara.
- Karma.

AE
- Transience:
  - accurate – nothing lasts, all is changing, we all die.
- Avidya:
  - accurate – ignorant of purpose in life
  - inaccurate – maybe there is no purpose of which to be ignorant.
- Brahman:
  - inaccurate – cannot be proved that we are all a part of Brahman.
- Reality:
  - accurate – we all see it differently so we don't know what it is.
  - inaccurate – it is real, it is not in our imagination (rejection of the concept of maya).

2. (continued)

- Gunas:
  - accurate – personalities are all different.
  - inaccurate – anybody can achieve spiritual perfection irrespective of personality.
- Samsara
  - inaccurate – no proof of its existence.
- Karma
  - accurate – words and actions can have consequences.
  - inaccurate – every thought does not have a consequence.

NB – these are just examples, the list is not exhaustive nor balanced – it is provided simply to give a broad outline of the kind of approach that may be taken by pupils.

SECTION 4: ISLAM

1. (a)
- The book is the Qur'an the word of Allah.
- It is the living word direct from Allah to humankind.
- It was given to Muhammad so of great importance.
- It is kept in a high place.
- It is never touched needlessly.
- Hands are always washed prior to touching.
- Kept wrapped in a cloth.
- Muslims attempt to learn it and memorise its content.

(b)
- Allah revealed himself through Muhammad.
- Therefore revealed himself to all Muslims.
- Muhammad therefore takes on a significant role.
- The Qur'an becomes the revealed word of Allah.
- All of life is directed by this revealed word.
- Muslims have a constant source of guidance.
- Qur'an the unchangeable word of Allah.
- No Muslim need go through life in ignorance.
- Every aspect of life is covered by this revealed word.
- Muslims are confident in their understanding of Allah.
- Allah has revealed himself to Muslims in a special way.
- Source of awareness of the ever present nature of Allah.

(c)
- It will give them strength knowing they are not alone.
- Will be an encouragement to keep the Five Pillars.
- A prompt for honest living.
- They will be aware that all life is a test on this earth.
- That Allah is a constant companion.
- They will use their freewill with thought of their actions.
- All actions will be measured by the word of Allah.

(d)
- Suffering is a part of every day life.
- It is linked to death and what will happen thereafter.
- Wrongdoing leads to suffering here and now.
- It also leads to suffering in the life after earthly life.
- Suffering is a punishment for sin.
- It is caused by the misuse of freewill.
- It happens less if Muslims do not question the will of Allah.

(d) (continued)
- It can be character building.
- Indifference of the needs of others can bring suffering to the individual.
- Life is a constant day to day test.
- Through suffering the Muslim is aware of the compassion of Allah.
- Theory of instrumentality.
- It could lead to a questioning of the purpose of life.
- It could be a strength.

(e) Maximum of 2 marks for description of heaven and hell
- There will be a great day when all will stand before Allah.
- Each individual and each nation will need to answer to Allah.
- There will be a record of the deeds of each individual.
- A similar record of the deeds of nations.
- Those who have lived in accord to the will of Allah will re rewarded.
- Those who have not will be punished.
- There will be a state of Barzakh between death and judgement.
- Belief in judgement is a basic principle in Islam.
- No Muslim is unaware of this forthcoming judgement so is a great prompt to a good life.

2.
- Salah is prayer.
- Prayer is performed five times per day.
- Times of prayer.
- Friday prayers at mosque of importance.
- Practices associated with prayer.
- Preparation for prayer.
- Prayer brings meaning to the life of the individual Muslim.
- It binds the individual to Allah in a strong way.
- It can offer support in times of doubt and uncertainty.
- Strength in times of sickness.
- Can bring routine and order to the individual.
- Binds them to the community of Islam.
- May be difficult especially in the western world.
- May separate from the wider community in the west.
- Bring a sense of brotherhood to the whole of Islam.
- Friday prayers will make one realise they are part of something much bigger.
- The coming together for prayer will strengthen the individual and the community.
- Prayer is one of the Five Pillars so without it Islam would be non existent.
- Centrality of the mosque and the community strengthened by prayer.
- Family life given more meaning and purpose.
- Bring understanding to the individual of their place in Islam.
- Could be argued that community of Islam is bigger than these things.
- That individuals could pray alone without all that Islam attaches to it.
- Belief in Allah more important.
- The teachings of Muhammad more important.

2008 Religious, Moral and Philosophical Studies Higher Paper 2 (cont.)

SECTION 5: JUDAISM

1. (a)
   - Led Jews out of slavery in Egypt to promised land.
   - Author of the Torah.
   - Established covenant with God.

   (b)
   - Creation stories – Adam and Eve.
   - God's dealings with Abraham and the patriarchs.
   - Ten plagues and the Exodus.
   - Return from Exile.
   - State of Israel.

   (c)
   - Becomes full member of the community.
   - Responsible for observing the commandments.
   - Reads portion of Torah in synagogue and puts on tefillin.
   - Rabbi addresses boy in his sermon.
   - Boy can now be counted as a member of the minyan.

   (d)
   - Give relevant examples of mitzvoth.
   - Mirrors split between religious and ethical mitzvoth.
   - Positive and negative commands.
   - Commandments about outward actions and inner thoughts.
   - Cover relationships with God and other people.

   (e)
   - Inclusion in Ten Commandments shows importance.
   - Emphasis on Shabbat ritual and family involvement.
   - Role of children in festivals (eg Pesach).
   - Importance of education and example within the family.
   - Role of the family in maintaining Jewish identity.

   (f)
   - Creation story – Adam and Eve punished for disobedience.
   - Disobedience by the people of Israel followed by suffering is a theme running through the Torah.
   - But there are other explanations of evil and suffering, eg Job, the suffering servant.
   - Holocaust has led to a wide range of explanations of evil and suffering.

2. **Briefly describe the relevant practices.**
   - Torah reading and study, Talmud and oral tradition.
   - Prayer and worship.
   - Ritual observance.
   - Repentance.
   - Charity and honesty.

   Arguments about their contemporary importance
   - Extent to which these practices are carried on today.
   - Differences between Orthodox and Reform approaches.
   - Difficulties and pressures faced by some Jews.
   - Jewish people as an example to the world.

SECTION 6: SIKHISM

1. (a)
   - The Creator – One and Universal.
   - God is Truth.
   - God is within as well as without.
   - Guru's grace – revealing God's Will (Hukam) through scriptures and through Chosen enlightened beings – Guru Nanak.

1. (b)
   - Guru Granth Sahib – living word of God (shabad).
   - Regarded as being as important as the 10 Guru's.
   - It is a living source and guide of inspiration for all stages of life.
   - Source of meditation and with understanding and action can take a Sikh closer to reunion with God.
   - Guru Granth Sahib has a daily role and a formal role during special occasions like birth and death.
   - Treated with great respect, given a place of central importance in the Gurdwara and at home.
   - Placed on a raised platform and covered with a canopy.
   - Worshippers fan the book with a chauri – as a sign of respect because this book contains the Word of God.
   - If a copy of the Granth is kept at home it must be given the same respect as if it were in a Gurdwara – a separate room, on a platform and it must be consulted daily.

   (c)
   - In order to achieve the goal of reunion with God, Sikhs must constantly develop their love for God by developing compassion for all God's creation.
   - All actions motivated by selflessness lead the soul/atma to God.
   - Action for personal gain is worthless.
   - They must atune their mind to God at all times – Gurmukh – God must be sounding in their minds at all times in order to be able to do God's Will (hukam).
   - Material wealth is unimportant.
   - Sharing – kara prashad at the Langar.
   - Sikh's accept their circumstances and stop looking for further ways to develop their own personal comfort.

   (d)
   - Humans have Free Will.
   - The ability to choose whether they follow God's Will or ignore it.
   - Service to others, following the Guru Granth Sahib and by the Guru's Grace are all combined to be ways to achieve union with God.
   - This choice will lead to happiness, however if they choose to focus on worldly goods and material possession they will fail to achieve their goal.
   - Create maya – illusion.
   - "wander aimlessly forever" through endless cycles of birth, life and rebirth.

   (e)
   2 marks for simply listing
   - Five Evils – sexual desire, anger, greed, emotional attachment and egoism.
   - Sexual desire – a desire to satisfy one's own need. No longer focuses on love for the other person. Sex should be between husband and wife and born out of love.
   - Anger – is all-consuming and destructive. It is harmful to yourself and to others. Leads to lack of self-control.
   - Greed – personal wealth and gain – Sikhs believe they should be content with what God has given them. If they focus on themselves they are no longer focused on God.
   - Emotional attachment makes one forget about God – family life is important but when attachment becomes excessive it is destructive and leads the soul away from God.

1. (continued)

- Pride (egoism) regarded as the worst of the Five Evils. It makes you treat others unfairly and badly. People like this forget that all their talents and gifts are from God and they attribute them to themselves. This leads them away from reunion with God.
- Pride leads to the haumai – because it makes people believe that they are the most important thing in life and this leads to self-centredness.
- By training their minds to focus on God at all times Sikhs believe that they can overcome the natural human impulses which create a barrier to reunion with God.

2.
- Khalsa formed by Guru Gobind Singh in 1699.
- Gobind Singh declared Khalsa to be his physical presence and that his spirit would live on in the Khalsa.
- Khalsa to live as "Saint-Soldiers".
- Panj Piaray – Five Beloved ones.
- Initiated by the Amrit ceremony.
- No caste system – everyone equal including women.
- 5K's – kara, kirpan, kesh, kachha and kangha.
- Kesh – uncut hair symbolizes that the Sikh is living in harmony with God.
- Kangha – a sign of spiritual discipline and purity as well as being practical for keeping their hair neat and tidy.
- Kara – steel bangle worn on right wrist – sign that they have made a commitment to serve God, who is One – it also reminds them of their faith at times of temptation.
- Kachha – cotton shorts or underwear, also a sign of purity.
- Kirpan – the sword symbolizes honour, courage and the fact that a Sikh must be ready to fight against injustice and defend those who need help.
- Each K is a practical reminder that they have made a commitment to follow a distinctive way of life.
- They show that members of the Sikh community are strongly bonded together.
- The 5 K's link every living member of the Khalsa with every Sikh warrior or Saint since 1699.
- In addition to this because they have very deep spiritual meaning, the removal of any one of the K's is considered to be a breach of the vows they have taken.
- If any of these vows are broken then the Sikh must go through the process of re-initiation.
- The symbols have become more powerful with every Sikh year that passes.

Official SQA answers to 978-1-84372-688-3
2006–2008